POP STYLES

VERMILION

I'm amazed you can't sing, Barrington. I mean, you look so absolutely super.

POP STYLES

TED POLHEMUS and LYNN PROCTER

VERMILION

London Melbourne Sydney Auckland Johannesburg

Also by Ted Polhemus and Lynn Procter
Fashion and Anti-Fashion

Also by Ted Polhemus
Social Aspects of the Body
The Body As A Medium Of Expression (co-editor)

Consultants:
D. M. Prior
Nigel di Talamo
Caroline Greville-Morris

Vermilion & Company

An imprint of the Hutchinson Publishing Group

17–21 Conway Street, London W1P 6JD

Hutchinson Publishing Group (Australia) Pty Ltd
16–22 Church Street, Hawthorn, Melbourne, Victoria 3122

Hutchinson Group (NZ) Ltd
32–34 View Road, PO Box 40–086, Glenfield, Auckland 10

Hutchinson Group (SA) Pty Ltd
PO Box 337, Bergvlei 2012, South Africa

First published 1984

© Ted Polhemus and Lynn Procter

Book designed by an act of G.O.D.

Set in Linotron 202 Times Roman and Helvetica Bold Roman Condensed
by Input Typesetting Ltd, London
Printed in Great Britain by Jolly & Barber Ltd, Rugby
and bound by Anchor Brendon Ltd, Tiptree, Essex

British Library Cataloguing in Publication Data

Polhemus, Ted
  Pop styles.
  1. Popular culture
  I. Title   II. Procter, Lynn
  306'.1   NX458

ISBN 0 09 155801 8

'But what about the music, man?'

Purists often complain that the pop world is polluted with the razzle dazzle trimmings of fashion. I first heard this grumble in Philadelphia around 1968 as *Time* and *Newsweek* focused on long hair and bell-bottoms, flower-power make-up and afro hair. I heard the same moans (with only the 'man' dropped to be replaced with some swearing), in London in 1977 among British punks who resented media focus on safety-pins and ripped t-shirts.

It's true that fashion is a heavy load for pop music to carry, but it got lumbered because of the nature of pop culture. Music is the highly marketable tip of the pop culture iceberg. Plastered over advertising hoardings, celebrated by television, newspapers, magazines and radio, pop music has inevitably come to represent pop and youth culture as a whole. Popular musicians have, therefore, rarely been able to concentrate solely on their music; as representatives of pop culture they have to dress the part.

When the earliest of our blues-based popular musicians – the blacks who had picked guitars and cotton in the American south – finally made it to Chicago, they discovered that looking flash was a key to success in a highly competitive field. Likewise, later big-band musicians such as Louis Jordan learned that time and money spent at the tailor, being fitted for an outlandish zoot suit, was a wise investment – even if it cut into rehearsal time. It's the same today; musicians who do not accept that creating and projecting a visual signature is part of the job may find work as backing musicians but stardom will often elude them.

Because our society thrives on perpetual change and because changing clothing styles are such an effective way of communicating the nature of these changes, we always need someone to stand in the spotlight to embody what's happening. In the past this role was played by film stars. Between Valentino's slicked back hair and Brando's leather jacket a lot of social changes were signalled by changing Hollywood fashions. But the television screen eroded the influence of the big screen and as the post-war baby boom entered adolescence 'teenagers' came into their own. The baton then passed from the Hollywood establishment to pop music as rock and roll swept all before it with Elvis Presley, Buddy Holly, Gene Vincent and all the others who have followed in their blue suede shoes.

As pop musicians became the representatives of pop culture as a whole, they became the focus of changing trends in all aspects of the visual arts. Album sleeve design and video direction are two especially important features of the package deal generated by today's pop personalities. But styles in clothing and adornment have a special significance for the rest of us; not many of us make stage sets or videos, work in graphic design or even make music but *we all wear clothes*. They are seldom as expensive, ornate, impractical or exaggerated as those worn on stage, but in our own ways we can recreate the spirit of whatever pop style we choose.

Every week small ads in the back pages of the music papers offer the opportunity to buy jewellery, t-shirts, trousers, badges, scarves, suits and shades which will link us with chosen heroes and heroines in ways which can be recognized by other fans. Thus pop styles provide, for those in tune, a common language of signs and symbols – bondage trousers, afghan coats, bovver boots, tight leather jeans, mini skirts, studded belts – which communicate tastes and philosophies, desires and dreams more effectively than any lonely hearts advert or computer dating questionnaire.

How ironic, then, that the styles which are so strongly associated with certain pop stars have usually originated not in the musician's mind's eye but among groups of creative young people in clubs, on the streets and in small shops and market stalls. More often the musician's role is one of exposing a good idea or design to a larger public rather than actually creating anything. There are cherished exceptions to this, but first we should consider what is undoubtedly the most typical source of pop styles – the street.

The classic development of any pop style is much the same as the classic development of any pop star – from the bottom to the top – and the average pop star keeps his original rags on his way up to riches. This may not literally be the case, money can buy new clothes for stage and street but, at least initially, most musicians stick with the same kind of style they enjoyed wearing before making it. If this is now exaggerated and glamourized then the process of stylistic dissemination to fans may be all the easier. The important thing is that the clothing styles which originate on the streets in little gangs and subcultures can suddenly be found on prime-time television, on giant billboards and on record sleeves in the windows of thousands of record shops throughout the world.

Toyah Willcox's hair creations are a case in point. Crazy colour was a street style which Toyah, like thousands of other kids, experimented with. Then, when success brought in the money to hire the best professional hairdressers, she used it as the basis for creating even more wonderful styles. But the idea remained the same from street to stage and back again.

The Beatle boot is another illustration of this. The British division of the beat generation which hung out in city coffee bars and cellar dives in the late fifties and early sixties were serious, sharp dressers. Loose tweed suits were out, all black and tight trousers were in, and a new type of pointed toe shoe with Italian styling and elastic sides instead of laces was essential to complete the look. The shoe, usually made to order by backstreet cobblers, grew higher and evolved into a boot, often with a Cuban heel. In Liverpool a few of the people who wore them were creating new and exciting music. The Mersey beat swept into the pop charts led by the Beatles, still wearing their boots, and soon kids all over the country and then the world wanted to copy them. Boot and shoe manufacturers were not averse to taking their money, and so the beat boot was reborn and christened the 'Beatle boot'. The fab four hadn't invented or designed it – they just had the sense not to completely discard their stylistic roots. With money in their pockets they ordered new pairs no doubt made by the best cobblers in the best leather – but they were beat boots all the same.

Continuing with the Beatles, we come across an interesting example of what is the least typical source of pop styles – high fashion. In the Beatles' Hamburg days of leather jackets and greased-back hair, it was their art school German friend Astrid Kirchherr who introduced them to the influence of *haute couture*. Astrid had made herself a collarless black jacket based on one in Paris designer Pierre

Clothing styles offer a cheap and immediate way to identify with pop heroes.
Opposite page, left hand row from top: 'The official Beatles sweater incorporating an exclusive and specially designed two-tone Beatle badge' from Weldons of Peckham Ltd. *New Musical Express* (NME), 1964. Collarless Beatle jacket from Aburtrim Ltd. DISC, 1964. Mersey boots from Mod Shoes ad in NME, 1964. Donovan jacket 'gives a man that "go anywhere, do anything" look. An outfit with a spice of adventure!' from Harry Fenton NME, 1965.
Centre row from top: 'You'll rave about this bag with its really great Beatles picture' from Milano Handbags NME, 1963. Carnaby Cavern 'We make suits for The Jam, Blondie, Specials, Joe Jackson, The Lambrettas and many others' ad including 'No. 1 . . . designed by Paul Weller of The Jam . . . based on the Beatle jacket of the sixties' SOUNDS, 1980. 'Adam Jacket . . . Superb value in black drill with yellow gold expandex printed braiding' from Mainline NME, 1981.
Right hand row from top: 'Granny collar detachable frill shirt' from Carnaby Cavern NME, 1969. Instant identification from Christopher Robin in SOUNDS featuring a choice of (from left) 3 Bowie outfits, Mod suit, Ska suit, Skinhead, Punk, Ted and Rock'a'billy outfits – a comprehensive guide to 1981 pop styles. Two NME ads for Pins 'n' Things – the Yazoo jacket from 1982, the Boy George smock and trousers from 1983

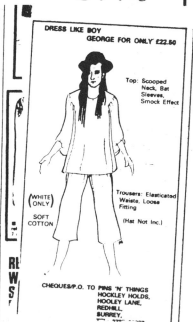
7

JULIE LONDON CALENDAR GIRL

EDSEL SPECTRA-SONIC-SOUND THE ULTIMATE IN HI FI

XED 109

JANUARY · FEBRUARY · MARCH · APRIL · MAY · JUNE · JULY · AUGUST · SEPTEMBER · OCTOBER · NOVEMBER · DECEMBER

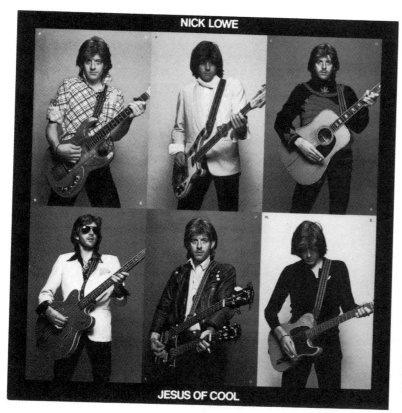

NICK LOWE

JESUS OF COOL

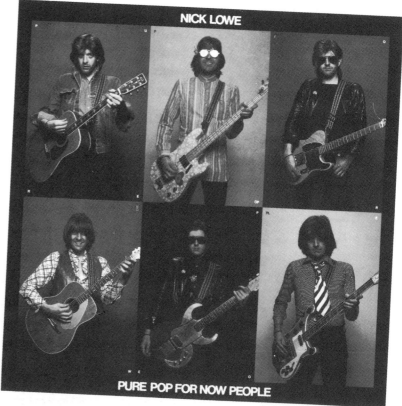

NICK LOWE

PURE POP FOR NOW PEOPLE

Cardin's recent collection and she ran up another for her boyfriend Stuart Sutcliffe, then the fifth Beatle. The others teased him: 'What are you doing in Mum's suit, Stu?' but later – after Stuart's death – when Brian Epstein decided they needed a cleaner image, they revived the collarless suit and, like their elastic-sided boots, it became an early symbol of the group. Clothing manufacturers pushed facsimiles into production and for years 'Beatle jackets' dominated the small ads in the music papers. Considering how long those ads ran, an awful lot of Beatle jackets must have been sold. The Beatles, however, soon moved on from Cardin-style suits. The symbolic repudiation of their street-style roots had never rested easily on their shoulders. Indeed throughout rock and roll's history, high fashion's inherent elitism has never really suited this music and its ideology. It was only in the Swinging London of the sixties, when high fashion itself had been knocked off its pedestal by the rise of boutiques and fresh young designers – led by Mary Quant in Chelsea's Kings Road and John Stephens in Carnaby Street – that rock musicians found they had anything in common with the fashion business. Since then there has been an alternative fashion force of young, non-establishment designers who have been able to effect easier relationships with the rock world; buying their clothes does not mean 'selling out'. Anthony Price, for example, although he has recently taken on a more elitist clientele, is widely respected in the pop world for his seventies designs for Roxy Music and his eighties suits for Bryan Ferry.

The partnership of Vivienne Westwood and Malcolm McClaren has achieved the closest blending of alternative fashion and pop music so far. Whilst running a shop called Sex (formerly known as Let It Rock and Too Fast To Live, Too Young To Die) on the Kings Road, Westwood and McClaren hit on the idea of starting up a rock band to serve as models for their designs and ideology. Previously designers had worked for pop people but not the other way round. Now this new band was even named The Sex Pistols to advertise the shop. The idea of creating their own pop figureheads was astonishingly successful and worked again with Bow Wow Wow. But aside from Price, Westwood/McClaren and a few others, whenever you stand back to take in the full sweep of rock and pop music history it becomes obvious that pop styles exist in a universe largely unaffected by designer based fashion.

More important is the third and final source of pop styles, those musicians who double as fountainheads of dress style innovation. While few pop stars design clothes in the sense that they sit hunched over a hot drawing-board, the history of pop music is richly veined with people who assimilate ideas from diverse sources and from them create an original style which is more than the sum of its parts. They use talented desigers as a conduit for their own inspiration. Renaissance men and women of the twentieth century, they provide us not only with music to dance to but also something to wear while we're dancing. They remind us that visual and musical styles, instead of being opposing forces, are in fact mutually enhancing partners in the project of giving a personal vision a public showing. A toast, then, to David Bowie, Grace Jones, Paul Weller, Spandau Ballet, ZZ Top, Gary Glitter, Liberace, Adam Ant, Boy George, Toyah, Elton John, Gary Numan, Sweet, Devo, The Tubes, Ozzy Osbourne, Ann Lennox and all the other sound and vision innovators. Cheers.

These musician/designers along with the alternative pop designers, the anonymous stylists of the

Some pop stars pick a style and stick to it while others enjoy playing the chameleon.
Opposite page, top: Julie London on 'Calendar Girl' from 1956. Bottom: Two copies of the same Nick Lowe album, 1978 – Left: The Scandinavian version 'Jesus of Cool'
Right: The American version 'Pure Pop For Now People' – the British version appropriately combines images from both

streets and the musicians who spread their ideas are challenging the role of *haute couture* as the arbiter of taste in dress. It is generally assumed that style changes originate on the catwalks of Paris, Milan, London and New York and then trickle down to the streets in diluted form. Not many years ago this was the case; Paris would decree whether hemlines would go up or down and the world would wait with baited breath, a pair of scissors in hand. Today things are very different, Paris designers can rarely get their acts together enough to agree whether hemlines this season are to be 6 inches above the knee or 12 inches below. Meanwhile the Japanese, Americans, British and Italians will probably be seeing things very differently.

But this anarchy of the catwalk is only one reason why people are paying less attention to *haute couture*. The other reason is the increasingly important role which pop styles play in influencing fashion. Except for the pope, royalty and a handful of politicians thrust into the spotlight by world events or scandal, pop musicians are the most photographed and visible human beings on earth. And the rising importance of pop promo videos and rock programmes on television have given pop stars even more exposure and more control over the way their image is presented. Pop is everywhere, you simply cannot avoid it, and where there's pop stars there's pop styles.

Haute couture simply cannot stand its ground against this saturation bombardment. Most people today know more about what this year's pop stars are wearing than they do about any top designer's new look. In the battle between 'Top Of The Pops', 'American Bandstand', 'The Tube' and MTV versus *Vogue*, *Gentleman's Quarterly* and *Womens Wear Daily*, the maverick contender looks like a force to be reckoned with.●

Above: Lone Groover cartoon by Tony Benyon from NME, 1981

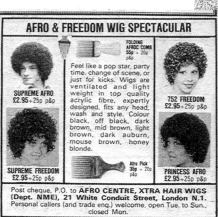

Until well into the sixties, most black performers were groomed to look as white as possible. Hair was straightened, greased, backcombed and sprayed until, with a bit of luck, it didn't look black and curly at all. But in the late sixties the Black Power movement emerged in the United States, 'radical chic' ruled, and suddenly for the young, liberal, fashionable or revolutionary Black was Beautiful. Hair which had for generations been constrained leapt free and grew naturally. While white kids grew theirs down, black kids grew theirs out. Old timers such as Muddy Waters could finally throw away the bottles of hair straightener. Some whites had curly perms and even those who couldn't grow their own could make it in an Afro Freedom Wig. For a while it looked as if every kid in the western world was trying out for the musical *Hair*.

Top right: The Rimshots, mid 1970s
Far right: Michael Jackson, 1974
Right: Ray Dorset, lead singer with Mungo Jerry who shot to fame after their success in the 1970 pop festival season
Centre: Ann Peebles in mid 1970s with a stunning bleached blonde afro
Top left: Afro and 'Freedom' wigs from Afro Centre advertisement in the NME, 1975

BAGGY TROUSERS

The history of pop styles is one of extreme pendulum swings. Although TIGHT TROUSERS with bulging crotches are an archetypal rock and roll garment, it was the extremely baggy trousered zoot suit which first established popular music as stylish in the extreme. But after getting as baggy as possible in the forties as a reaction to wartime cloth restrictions and then settling down in the fifties to wide legged pegs cut in at the ankle, baggy trousers were challenged by the new drainpipes and then body-hugging flares worn by both sexes. But bags with wide straight legs caught on again by the early seventies and pegs became essential dress for British male Northern Soul fans, resurfacing among the New Romantics in the late seventies. In between, the baggy style had been taken to astounding extremes by David Bowie in ballooning trousers known as 'Bowies' which kept many a tailor in work sewing pleats for the Thin White Duke's many fans and imitators.

Clockwise from top left:
Spencers ad from NME, 1983
Tartan hipster Oxford bags on The Gorillas' 1976 single
Bowie in Bowies, 1975
Baxby Fashions House ad for Bowies NME, 1981
Madness even wrote a song about them – ad for 'Baggy Trousers' from NME, 1980
30" bottom baggies ad from Kellies-Eye Co. NME, 1974
Baggies from Wrider Jean Co. NME, 1974

Derived from both military and American athletic styles, the bomber jacket might seem too practical to make it as a pop style. Yet it became *the* jacket to wear with Oxford Bags (see BAGGY TROUSERS). Its simple styling made it suited to decoration and so the bomber was taken up by bands who used the back for their logo or name. Each tour by a major band soon had its own tour jacket worn by the roadies in place of a badge or pass, and kept as a souvenir with the added status of 'proving' that the wearer had worked with and really *knew* the band. Tour jackets were considered quite hip in the super-group days of the seventies but by the eighties they came to be seen as tacky.

Clockwise from top right:
Status Quo in matching 1984 tour jackets and – of course – denim jeans. It's hard to believe that the Quo once went in for paisley prints and brocade kaftan-style jackets
Fabmale ad from NME, 1967
Command Surplus Centre Ltd. ad NME, 1968
Leo Sayer in Chinese embroidered bomber jacket
Two ads for George Michael NME, 1974

BOOTS

Before the sixties, boots were used largely as practical, protective footwear – Wellingtons, riding boots, motorbike boots. For a few they had fetishistic overtones but they had not been in fashion for decades. While elastic-sided boots, eventually known as Beatle boots, developed their own following amongst men (see INTRODUCTION) Mary Quant followed Courreges by introducing fashion boots for women. They caught on in a big way in the pop world and inspired at least two hit records – Honor Blackman (then Kathy Gale of 'The Avengers' TV series) made 'Kinky Boots' and Nancy Sinatra exposed the style with her international hit 'These Boots Are Made For Walkin' ' in the mid-sixties. Since then all kinds of boots have become pop styles. Multicoloured leather or wooden-soled boots of the early seventies, which developed into those incredible platforms, deserve a special mention – how else could would-be pop stars carry their own 6-inch high stage around with them? Elton John as the Pinball Wizard in *Tommy* and Fee Waybill of The Tubes were not even satisfied with 6-inch heels. Since then British 'Oi' and skinhead groups have made a cult of Dr Martens 'bovver boots' and punks have introduced complex, almost fetishistic versions of zipped and buckled motorbike boots. Today, boots are not only fashionable but there's also a different style for every taste.

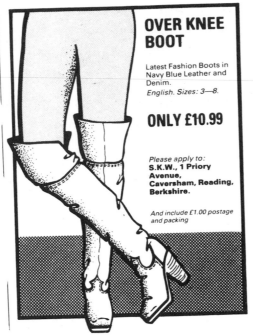

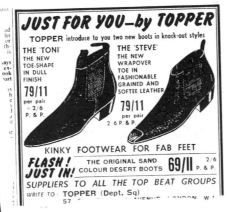
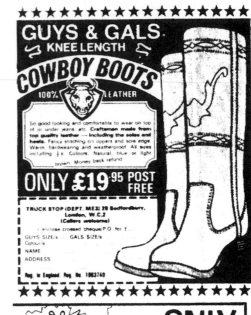
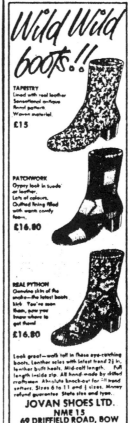
Top left: Thigh boots from S.K.W. in NME, 1977
Above: 'Guys & Gals' cowboy boots from Truck Stop NME, 1976
Right: Shelly's present their 'Christmas Top Ten Hits' – ''Still at number one'' Chelsea boots with elastic inserts, 'at number two a new entry' pilot boots in 'black or stone washed (worn look) leather . . . and at three' biker boots. Ad in NME, 1983
Centre: The 'triple decker platform' Trebler and the Wood-e with 3½" wooden heel from Tabco NME, 1974
Bottom row from left: 'Ringo' beat boots 'The latest rave' from Regis Shoes Ltd. NME, 1964
'Kinky footwear for fab feet' beat boots 'in knock-out styles' from Topper ad in NME, 1964
Left: Boots in 'sensational antique floral pattern Tapestry', 'gypsy look in suede or leather' and 'real Python' from Jovan Shoes Ltd. NME, 1971

Top left: Bovver boots with 'heavy cleated commando screw-on soles' and 'internal steel toe-cap' and Dr Martens classic bovver boot both from Gregory Shoes ad in NME, 1981
Top centre: Ladies' boot from Melanddi ad in SOUNDS, 1983
Centre: 'Rocker platforms' with 4" heels from Soul Organisation NME, 1974
Top right: Cuban heel beat boots with 'specially constructed height now in fashion with "beat" trends', from La Mode ad in NME, 1964
Below: Two ads from Bloggs in NME, 1977, for 'The rebel boot . . . made especially for anti-establishment heroines!' and other 'riotous creations for punk sisters' including 'Trouble Makers' with 'cult ankle chain with safety-pin buckle — boots to dictate by' and Strutters 'for chicks who don't give a damn' 'Anarchistically priced'?
Bottom right: Fee Waybill of The Tubes as Quay Lude — the definitive parody of the drug crazed super-star, complete with outrageous glasses, tight snakeskin jeans and *enormous* platform boots

BRACES

Known in America as suspenders, braces were designed to hold up trousers in the days when they didn't fit tightly at the waist. Whether it's high-waisted zoot suits or those baggy tweed affairs our grandfathers used to wear, belts just don't work on all trousers and, as male tailoring again diversifies away from pegs and jean-type trousers, there are practical reasons for the return of braces. However, for most people who wear them they are just a stylish accessory and, like wearing belts with tight jeans, they are decorative rather than functional. In these cases they symbolize old-fashioned traditionalism and/or working-class roots.

Left: The Beverley Sisters appearing in their 1950s TV series
Below: Judge Dread and band on 'Last of the Skinheads'
Bottom left: Chas Hodges and Dave Peacock – London folk heroes through their 'Rockney' music – go for a paddle at Margate
Bottom centre: Duffo *en deshabille*
Bottom right: John Keeble of Spandau Ballet

Chas&Dave MARGATE

Top left: Mik Sweeney of Classix
Nouveaux
Bottom left: Annette Peacock on
'X-Dreams'
Main picture: Ian Dury strips off
to join the keep fit craze on
'New Boots and Panties!!'

17

BROTHEL CREEPERS

These delightfully named, shoes with thick, soft crepe soles are the definitive Blue Suede Shoes which we were warned not to step on. The colour isn't really important, the key factor is that in the fifties even the most conventional shoes suggested that a man was racy and unreliable if they were made of suede. These silent wonders were so different from respectable, shiny, leather lace-ups that they set the wearer apart from the crowd and, for the British Teddy Boy, they have for the last twenty-five years been *the* thing to wear with a quiff, drape jacket and drainpipes.

THE BEST OF CHESS CHECKER CADET

doo-wop

Let Me In
— Sensations
Peanut Butter
— Marathons
Knee Socks
— Ideals
Sincerely
— Moonglows
MTY LTT
— Dream Kings
I'm So Young
— Students
Long Lonely Nights
— Lee Andrews and the Hearts
False Alarm
— Revels
I'll be Home
— Flamingos
Over the Mountain, Across the Sea
— Johnny & Joe
Happy Happy Birthday Baby
— Tune Weavers
Been so Long
— Pastels
Tippety Top
— Rays
White Cliffs of Dover
— The Blue Jays

CREEPERS
Buckle and Lace. Suede.
Red, Blue, Black.
Real Crepe Soles.

CREEPERS
THE STYLISH ONES

Contact Bob Smith, Denson, 2-44 Kingsland Rd, ...on E2. Tel: 01-739 7551

DENSON

Top left: Detail from rock 'n roll revival group Showaddywaddy's single 'Goody Goody', 1982
Top right: The Best of Chess 'Doo-wop' sleeve
Above: 'Suede creeper on crepe base with 1¾ in heel' from Orpheus ad in NME, 1974
Right: 'Pointed toe buckle creeper . . . Available in Black, Red, Blue, Grey or Purple Suede' from Melanddi ad in NME, 1983
Far right: Buckle and lace creepers from Denson NME, 1978
(See also BOOTS)

BULLET BELTS

The bullet belt started off as part of the singing cowboy look as worn by Gene Autry, but it never caught on with the public until it was popularized as the ultimate heavy metal accessory in the early seventies. Conveying an anti-love-and-peace message, this surge of interest partly marked the end of hippy rock and the beginning of modern heavy metal. Bullet belts also convey an idea of the musician as Mexican-bandit-come-guerilla-fighter, but the carnage is limited to eardrums.

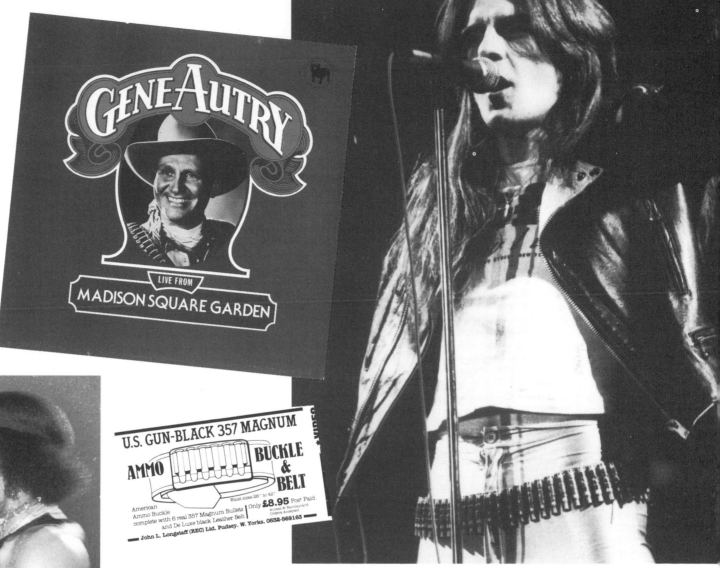

Gene Autry

LIVE FROM
MADISON SQUARE GARDEN

U.S. GUN-BLACK 357 MAGNUM

AMMO   **BUCKLE & BELT**

American Ammo Buckle complete with 6 real 357 Magnum Bullets and De Luxe black Leather Belt

Waist sizes 28" to 42"   Only **£8.95** Post Paid. Access & Barclaycard Orders Accepted

John L. Longstaff (REC) Ltd. Pudsey, W. Yorks. 0532-569163

Top left: Gene Autry, the first artist to bring country music to a mass audience, shown here with Mexican bandit style over-the-shoulder bullet belt
Top right: Biff of Saxon
Right: Motorhead, looking even meaner than Gene Autry
Above: Bullet belt 'complete with 6 real 357 Magnum Bullets' from John L. Longstaff (REC) Ltd. SOUNDS, 1982
Left: Grandmaster Flash looking heavy

CAPES

In the sophisticated fifties female singers were often photographed arriving at airports in mink capes – whatever the weather. In the mid-sixties short police-type capes were popular as part of the craze for eccentric and colourful military uniforms. This developed into the hippy fondness for Moroccan robes, Mexican ponchos, romantic long cloaks and useful blankets worn to pop festivals. In the Glam '70s a new kind of cape – all shiny and flash – hit the pop concert stage. Sinister, theatrical and suitable for dramatic swirling effects, it was a real must for the aspiring pop star.

Left: Steve Priest of the Sweet in glam lurex cape and make-up, mid 1970s
Top left: Jock Macdonald of the Bollock Brothers shows off the satin lining of his cape for the single 'Drac's Back', 1983
Top right: Shawn Phillips on 'Second Contribution' in full-length hippy cape, 1969
Above: Scott McKenzie, without flowers in his hair, in velvet cape, 1967

Above: From the glamorous days before rock 'n' roll took over the pop world, the most prominent clothing ad in NME in 1956 was for Barbican Supplies' 'mink coney fur cape'
Left: Wool cape from A. Woodruff & Co. Ltd.
NME, 1969

Left: Paul Stanley of Kiss in silver cape, late 1970s
Top right: 'The unisex gear for cool happenings and draughty demos!' from GR & DC Enterprises NME, 1969
Centre right: Cord cape from Carnaby Maid, DISC, 1968
Above: Dee D. Jackson, 1978

21

Caps come in many types with different associations – smart uniforms, innocent schoolboys, committed Rastafarians, cheeky barrow boys, poor workers, etc. They can be easily adapted by a pop star and used to effectively communicate in just a head and shoulders photo.

Michael Jackson
Got To Be There

HMA 200

Donovan
Catch The Wind

Electronically Created STEREO

HALLMARK

Opposite page:
Clockwise from top left:
Michael Jackson, 1972
Donovan's characteristic protest singer image, 1965
Fans could copy him – and get a free photo of their hero – in caps
and jackets from M. & B. Linens ad in NME, 1965
Fans of another star later obtained 'Genuine replicas of style as
worn by Donny Osmond – in super quality scarlet velvet' from
Cards & Posters NME, 1973
Marc Bolan on 'Cat Black', a 1981 re-issue of 1966 material
'Marlon Brando cap – black vinyl cap, fully lined with eagle badge,
studs and chains – macho, macho – do it!!' from a
Printout Promotions ad in SOUNDS, 1982
A 'macho, macho' Gina X does it, 1980

This page:
Clockwise from above:
Bruce Springsteen, 1981
Madness in traditional working men's flat caps, 1982
Joboxers with a similar rough-and-ready, streetwise image, 1983
Bob Marley on 'Rastaman Vibration', 1976
Alannah Currie of the Thompson Twins, known for her enormous
Beau Geste-style cap, 1983

COWBOYS

YOU GOTTA HAVE LOVE IN YOUR HEART
I WONDER WHERE WE'RE GOING
CALL ME
ONE MORE BRIDGE TO CROSS
IF YOU COULD SEE ME NOW
I'LL TRY NOT TO CRY
I'M GLAD ABOUT IT

Perhaps in this day and age we should speak of cow*persons*, as increasingly it is female pop stars who have taken on the trappings of the cowboy (see Carlene Carter FRINGE, Judy of the Bellestars TIES). Only a few years ago, however, this was the preserve of male country and western singers who saw in the garb of the cowboy a way of underlining their rural, as opposed to urban, inclination. This did a lot for some singers but very little for our understanding of the original cowpokes who were generally too poor to be flash.

EDDIE NOACK

ACE Records

Opposite page:
Top: The Supremes and The Four Tops looking real mean on the sleeve of 'The Return of The Magnificent Seven', 1971
Bottom left: Eddie Noack, 1950s Texan hillbilly singer and songwriter for Hank Snow and George Jones – photo from Ace's 'Eddie Noack'
Bottom right: Dan Peek, religious country singer, late 1970s
This page:
Right: An 'authentic Western shirt' which would be coveted by many fashionable people today, as advertised in NME in 1952
Top right: Elvis Presley, Scotty Moore and Bill Black from 1954–5 when they were touring the southern circuit – which included The Louisiana Hayride radio programme and the *Grand Ole Opry* – singing and performing in rockabilly style
Bottom right: Jim Reeves pictured on RCA's re-issue of his 1954 Abbott recordings
Below: Johnny Cash on 'Old Golden Throat' complete with string tie, quiff and gun, late 1950s

THUNDER IN THE MOUNTAINS — THUNDER IN THE MOUNTAINS

Toyah

Left: Toyah Willcox, 1981
Right: Roy Wood of Wizzard,
early 1970s
Far right top: Barbie Wilde of
Shock, 1983
Far right bottom: Exploited. A
detail from 'Troops of
Tomorrow', 1983

26

Perhaps the most important pendulum swing in the history of pop styles is that between nature and artifice. One of the best ways to join the against-nature school of thought is to dye your hair a bright colour or better still a whole collection of colours which nature never intended to appear on the head of a human being. Historical examples are few, however, as the technology has only been widely available a short time. Only impermanent vegetable dyes were available before the seventies and it was punks who first combined an anti-natural attitude with the new chemicals. Special credit therefore goes to Wee Willie Harris who caused a furore in the fifties when he dyed his hair so pink it dripped down his collar in the rain, Roy Wood who fronted Wizzard behind a mass of multicoloured locks and of course David Bowie. (See MAKE-UP). Ultimately, however, the first prize must go to post-punk Toyah Willcox who with dyes and hair spray has resculpted her head into a homage to artifice which even the most daring of science fiction films have failed to equal.

CROPS AND CREW CUTS

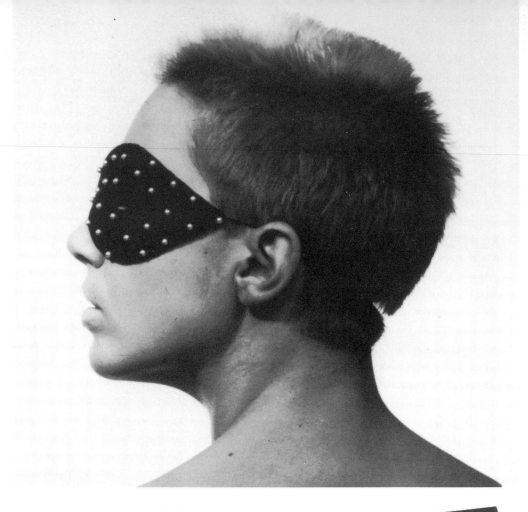

Rock and roll's prevailing long-haired rebel image has had its counterpoint not only in the cropped, short-haired rebel look but also in the respectable, clean-cut, nice-guy style. The short-haired rebel is relatively recent, derived primarily from British skinheads and punks. The acceptable face of rock and roll, however, has been with us ever since it dawned on America that, as the rock and roll teen menace didn't look like going away, the only way to combat it was to appropriate it for the forces of good. The irony is that Elvis Presley put up no resistance to Uncle Sam's army barbers as they removed the last remains of the greased quiff which had horrified middle America almost as much as those pelvic gyrations. The respectable hoped that the rest of the long-haired hordes would be forced to join the likes of Pat Boone, The Four Freshmen and The Crew Cuts.

But soon the long-hairs fought back and kept a grip on the pop world until the late seventies when everyone (except the heavy metal and the new glam mobs) raced to the hair dressers to get it chopped. Some, taking their cue from skinheads and suedeheads took things as far as possible short of sporting SHAVED HEADS.

Today rock and roll subversion has had the last laugh with gender bending female pop stars in the same hair cuts which once reassured America that the devil didn't have all the best tunes.

Left: The Moods, a Texan high school band from the early 1960s in flat tops and formals
Top: Ann Lennox of The Eurythmics, 1983
Above: The Crack, winners of the 1982 'Battle of the Bands' in contemporary versions of traditional skinhead crops
Right: Grace Jones' ultimate flat top from 'Living My Life', 1982

The DA or Duck's Arse was, and amongst remaining enclaves of Teddy Boys still is, the rearview equivalent of the quiff. Through a miracle of cutting and combing, a parting is created which resembles the folded wings of a duck with, as an optional extra, a small tail at the nape of the neck.

Illustration from the back of Dave Taylor's 'Jive, Jive, Jive'

THE TEMPTATIONS
SURFACE THRILLS

KEVIN ROWLAND & DEXYS MIDNIGHT RUNNERS
"LET'S GET THIS STRAIGHT FROM THE START" & "OLD"

Rock and roll espouses the virtues of the rough and ready and denim is the perfect symbol of this. If you look through the earliest issues of the *New Musical Express* you will find that the only clothing ads are for fake mink CAPES and flashy JEWELLERY, but as soon as the words 'rock and roll' appear we find the first ad for denim clothes. It was the fabric for a new classless, transatlantic world. Kids wanted jeans as much as the new music. In Britain until the mid-sixties a pair of genuine American jeans were a real status symbol, almost as they are behind the Iron Curtain today. As few were imported, most people had to make do with cheaper copies which just didn't fit right. But in the late sixties the floodgates opened and denim swept through Britain until every young person in the country, and lots of older ones too, seemed to be dressed in that particular blue. Martians landing in 1976 would have been convinced that earth people were blue and fading fast. By then denim clothes had swamped the small ads in the musical papers; *everything* was made out of it.

And then the bubble burst. It had a lot to do with the emergence of punks and their scorn for all things tainted by the 'hippy' world. A conflict of cultures was inevitable when the *Tommy* ad shown here was still running in the *NME* the week in 1976 when the Sex Pistols' swearing outraged a British television audience. Glam rock with its satins and sequins had put a small dent into the denim revolution but soon a majority style was coralled into a defensive minority.

An eighties rockabilly revival resurrected denim and we have now seen its rediscovery in the ripped and torn 'hard times' look which recreates and parodies the original rock and roll rebel image.

Previous page
Top left: John Cougar Mellencamp, 1983
Top right: The Temptations in their own 'designer' jeans, 1983
Bottom left: Peter Kaukonen of Jefferson Starship exemplifies the late 1960s/early 1970s patched denim look
Bottom centre: Kevin Rowland in vagabond chic dungarees, 1982
Bottom right: Cher in transition from the hippy 1960s to the glam 1970s
This page
Top left: Status Quo epitomise the denim mania of the mid 1970s
Bottom left: A Tommy ad from NME, 1976, shows how you too can look like Status Quo
Bottom right: Where it all started – Lybro advertisement from DISC 1963

DRAPE JACKETS

In Britain Ted or Teddy is an abbreviation of Edward; Teds or Teddy Boys are British rock and rollers who derive their name from the Edwardian dandy styles (after Edward VII) which they affect. This manner of dress had begun as the badge of upper-class students at Oxford and Cambridge, but post-war working-class British lads, thumbing their noses at their parents' belief that you should keep to your station in life, adopted the elegantly tailored draped coat of the Oxbridge set. But the kids listened to American rock and roll, and when their heroes came to Britain to perform they must have been somewhat taken aback by what has (until the Japanese joined in) always been a distinctly British phenomenon – groups of lads all clad in long jackets in rich fabrics with the collar in a contrasting colour. Individually tailored at great expense, a drape jacket or SUIT is every Teddy Boy's most prized possession. Like the mod's parka, the drape was popularized by the fans rather than the musicians – who only adopted the style when various rock and roll revivals took hold and groups such as Showaddywaddy looked for inspiration not to the dress of the original musicians but to the fans who had never hung up their drapes.

'Teddy Boys convinced us we didn't want nothing to do with classical rock and roll, it was so mindless. . . . They thought if you didn't wear a drape suit it wasn't classical rock and roll. But no singer ever dressed like that. Chuck Berry never wore a drape suit.'

Wilko Johnson, Dr Feelgood

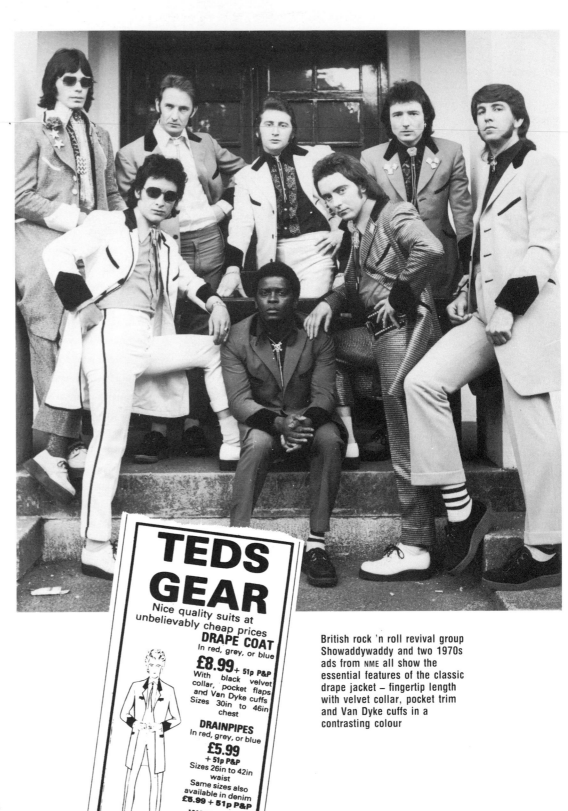

British rock 'n roll revival group Showaddywaddy and two 1970s ads from NME all show the essential features of the classic drape jacket – fingertip length with velvet collar, pocket trim and Van Dyke cuffs in a contrasting colour

DREADLOCKS

Although originating in the tenets of the Rastafarian religion, dreadlocks have become an important pop style disseminated by the wide impact of reggae. Like the afro, the effect is natural in the sense that black, kinky hair, if left to grow long enough, will matt into strands. Plaiting isn't necessary, combing is impossible, washing and oiling are time consuming but are the only upkeep required. White pop people have tried to get in on the act but it is not easy. Molten candle wax is dripped onto false hair pieces entwined with strands of growing hair to bind them together. Once accomplished, the process can only be reversed by cutting it all off. Real Rastafarians are often none too flattered by the imitation – Kate of Haysi Fantazee has even been assaulted in the street.

Top: Bob Marley, the original and definitive dreadlocked superstar on 'Kaya', 1978
Below left: Eddy Grant
Below centre: Kate and Jeremy of Haysi Fantayzee
Below right: Marilyn
Overleaf: Big Youth with all the rasta trappings

BOB MARLEY & THE WAILERS

CALLING YOUR NAME Marilyn

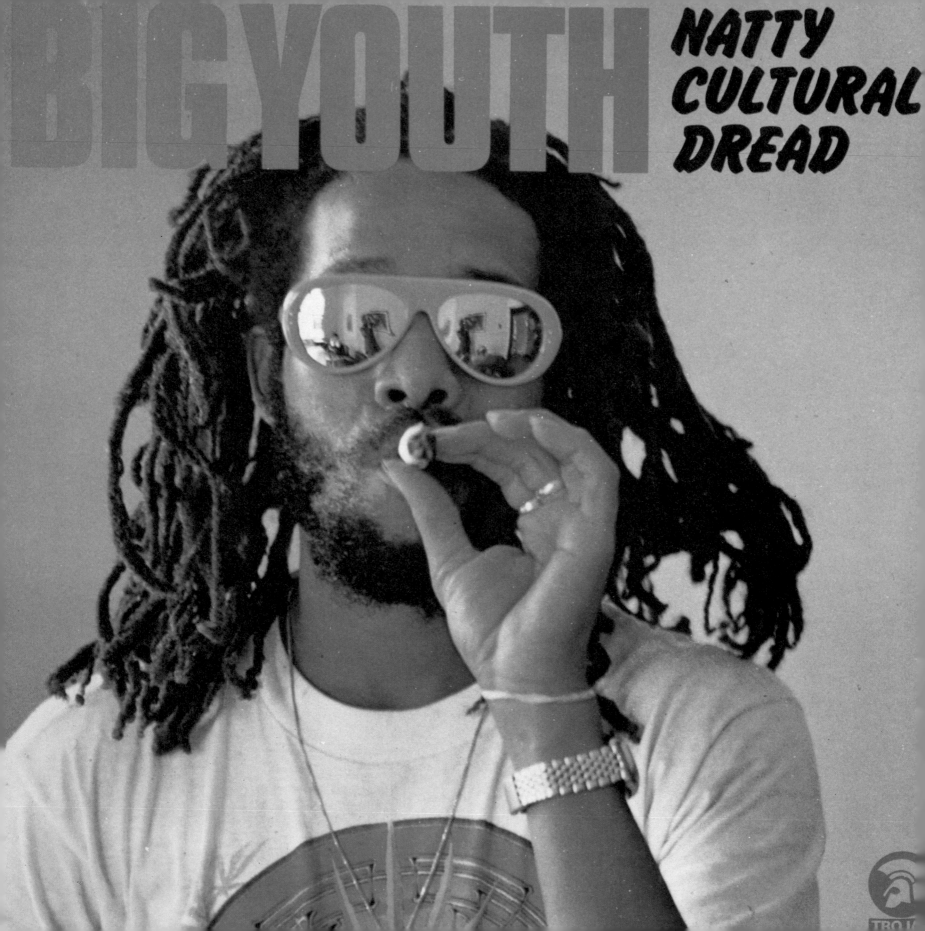

A time-consuming decorative process, embroidery is associated with either a lot of time and patience or a lot of money. In the case of a typical pop star it's probably the latter – we really cannot believe that Porter Wagoner sits up late in the evenings finishing the cactii and other extraordinary designs on his suit. But a lot of fans have spent hours embroidering references to their pop idols onto their clothes.

Country and western style embroidery is flash and expensive but a cheap alternative was found by hippies and subsequent travellers in third world countries. This has appeared on DENIM, FLARES and various ETHNIC styles from Indian kaftans to Chinese jackets to African prints.

Left: Hank Snow in a 1950s example of classic country and western embroidery
Top: John Denver in folksy embroidered denim, 1976
Far right: Porter Wagoner personifies the country and western superstar on 'Porter and Dolly' – that's Parton of course – 1980
Near right: An alternative style of embroidery – "Tomorrow's shirt today!" – for the swingers reading DISC in 1968

COOL IT – with this NEW EMBROIDERED SHIRT!

WHETHER YOU'RE WAY IN OR WAY OUT IT'S A MIND BLOWER

This is tomorrow's shirt today! Beautifully made in finest poplin with top to bottom front embroidered Anglais Lace with deep set collar. Colours: White, Lemon, Pink, Blue, Green, Orange, Lilac. Please

ONLY 99/6

35

Below: Elton John on 'Rocket Man' single doing a passable imitation of Porter Wagoner, 1972
Centre top: ZZ Top in the days before their beards totally dominated their image. Do ZZ Top, Elton and Porter Wagoner share the same tailor?
Centre bottom: Andy Scott in delicately embroidered shirt
Right hand column from top:
Embroidered loons and waistcoat from Renaissance ad in NME, 1974
White embroidered kurta from Shapes ad NME, 1979
Embroidered shirt and flares from Postal Boutique ads NME, 1973

In pop's early days bebop, rock and roll and surfer styles developed directly from the music's environment. In the mid-sixties, however, particularly with the rising influence of folk music, people began consciously to look to other times and places for inspiration and a way of making some sort of statement of solidarity with romantic peasants and oppressed ethnic groups. Afghan coats, kaftans, kurtas, ponchos, Tibetan hats, Mexican sweaters, buckskin jackets, Navaho jewellery and much more began to appear in smart shops and street markets and also on the backs of pop stars and fans. (Ironically, with the significant exception of Jimi Hendrix, black musicians of the same period were wearing archetypal western dress in the form of tuxedos and evening gowns). Our tendency to look to third world countries in search of bright ideas continues and in the eighties we have turned especially to black Africa.

Left: Brigit Novik goes mid-European peasant
Above: Robin Trower goes Moroccan
Below: Kaftan East ad from NME, 1973 at the height of the post-hippy ethnic era. By this time mass imports from around the world allowed everyone in the West — male and female, young and old — to identify with the now fashionable Third World

EBENEZER OBEY

the slits

Cut

This page
Top left: The real thing
– African musician
Ebeneezer Obey
Bottom left: Denny Laine of
the Moody Blues and Wings
goes late hippy ethnic
Top right: Punk group The
Slits go native in 1979
Bottom right: Post punk
group Access cleverly
parody the Slits' parody of
jungle chic
Opposite page
Syreeta discovers her
roots and shows Bo Derek
how, 1980

beef

Access

KING

Sunny Adé and his African Beats

Segun Ilori: Guitar

Michael Babalola: Maracas

Matthew Olojede: Vocals

Sunny Adé: Lead Guitar, Vocals

Femi Owomoyela: Vocals

Shina Abiodun: Congos

SYNCHRO SYSTEM ♪ SYNCHRO SYSTEM ♪ SYNCHRO SYSTEM ♪ SYNCHRO SYSTEM ♪ SYNCHRO SYSTEM ♪ SYNCHRO SYSTE

Niyi Falaye: Vocals

John Akpan: Rythm Guitar

Rasaki Aladokun: 2nd Talking Drums

Jacob Ajakaye: Vocals

Gani Alashe: Shekere

Bob Ohiri: Guitar

SYNCHRO SYSTEM ♪ SYNCHRO SYSTEM ♪ SYNCHRO SYSTEM ♪ SYNCHRO SYSTEM ♪ SYNCHRO SYSTEM ♪ SYNCHRO SYSTE

Fatoke Abiodun: Agogo

Alhaji Timmy Olaitan: Lead Talking Drums

Jelili Lawal: Bass

Demola Adepoju: Steel Guitar

Tunde Demiola: Vocals

Moses Akanbi: Drums

Left: Sunny Adé (top left) goes Western while his African Beats stick to the real thing – traditional Nigerian dress.
This page clockwise from top left:
Savanna go Mexican
Incantation also get into ponchos but with the flavour of the Andes
Anna goes for the ubiquitous kaftan
Tane Cain goes American Indian
'Kinky Kaftans, a must for all you ravers' complete with '2in. standfast Mandarin Collar' on offer from NME as early as 1967
Jane Aire goes for a far-Eastern look

FEATHERS

Throughout history, people have used feathers for decoration and there is no reason why pop people shouldn't do so too. Traditionally signifying power and prestige, they provide the musician with a valuable armoury of symbols, from the successful hunter or warrior brave to the charismatic shaman or ritual leader.

CHARLEY SINGS
Everybody's Choice

CHARLEY PRIDE

This page
Top: Charley Pride, 1982
Bottom: Todd Rundgren, mid 1970s
Right: Eno of Roxy Music, 1973
Opposite page
Left: Aretha Franklin, early 1980s
Top: Dana Gillespie, late 1970s
Bottom: The Supremes, early 1970s

THE SUPREMES
FEATURING
MARY WILSON

FLOY JOY
STONED LOVE
BAD WEATHER
NATHAN JONES
UP THE LADDER TO THE ROOF

GREATEST HITS

SUPREMES

FLARES

Of all the styles in this book, flares currently provoke the most ridicule. Once it might have been tattoos or peroxide but today's dirty word is flares. Record company press officers snatch pictures from your hand and musicians lie through their teeth that they never wore them. But everyone over the age of thirty stands indicted. Their banishment was swift – almost overnight in the late seventies – but their coming was gradual. In 1964 adverts began to appear in the music papers for flared trousers which, in the light of later excesses, appear quite subtle. The inspiration for trousers which are tight at the top and loose at the bottom is obscure. Sailors' bell-bottoms may have a lot to answer for. At any rate, once this style had gained hold there was – as is always the case with truly successful pop fashions – no constraint on excess. Triangular inserts from the knee down, often in contrasting fabric, became a fashionable and cheap way of converting old trousers to the new rage. Hippy musicians sported bell-bottoms which dragged on the ground and frayed. 'Loons' were tight enough at the top to cause speculation in the papers about the fertility of the next generation. Meanwhile the chevron split-knee design was introduced to make even wider flares possible. When glam rock peaked, perhaps because things could go no further, flares disappeared like dinosaurs. Today they are almost extinct but tomorrow, who knows, we may all be crawling round our attics hunting for those treasured antiques.

44

Top row from left:
Portobello Post and Sujo ads from NME, 1972
Three Carnaby Cavern ads from NME, 1970 in brocade, Trevira and sateen 'as supplied to many famous groups . . . now offered for the first time to the public'
Centre row from left:
'Split knee brushed denims' from Tradewinds NME, 1972
'They're the latest! BELL-BOTTOM JEANS styled for the 'shake'. Made from top quality blue English denim with fringe round trouser bottoms to accentuate rhythmic movement. Another Fab creation from CHARMWEAR' NME, 1964
Postal Boutique NME, 1973
Sujo NME, 1973
Bottom row from left:
The Chi-Lites, mid 1970s
Asterisk NME, 1972

FRINGES

Cowboys probably stole the idea from American Indians. Like the 1920s flappers and 1960s go-go dancers, pop people relish them for their effect in accentuating movement. Beaded hair (see Syreeta in ETHNIC) has much the same effect. Fringes have a life of their own – a phenomenon emphasized by sixties strobe lighting.

"I Will Always Love You"

Dolly

Country and Western style fringe, shown here by Dolly Parton (left), Rick Nelson (bottom left) and Carlene Carter (overleaf) is one of the oldest pop styles. Fashionable versions emerged in 1969–70 exemplified by Grace Slick of Jefferson Airplane/Starship (top far left) and Roger Daltrey (p.46)

Fans could in 1970 emulate their fringed heroes with the help of ads in NME (above) and DISC (left). As these ads show, the style had now shifted from the establishment cowboy to the oppressed Indian. Post-punk ripped cotton fringes as worn by Bonnie Tyler (bottom centre) came in in the late 1970s. Whatever styles come and go, the dramatic effect of moving fringes will always be part of rock 'n roll – see Ozzy Osbourne (centre top), late 1970s

Top: Carlene Carter, 1980
Above: Dee Snider of
Twisted Sister, 1983
Right: One of the classic
images of the pop festival
era, Roger Daltrey of The
Who around 1970

46

FURS AND FAKES

Bryan Ferry

Furs are a magical link between the primitive savage and the sophisticated city dweller. Pop people use them as symbols of savagery and of wealth. But more appropriate to rock's essential vulgarity is the brash and obvious fakery of fun furs. For the oldest rockers and the newest post-punks these fakes can provide a deliberate tackiness which is in the finest spirit of rock and roll. They save on killing animals too.

Left: Bryan Ferry of Roxy Music, 1972
Right: Marion Sauva of The Doll, 1979
Below: Smokey Robinson, 1980
Below right: Annabella Lwin, 1982

Top left: Keith Moon in fake fur fancy dress
Centre left: Frankie Laine in rugged sheepskin jacket
Bottom left: Max Splodge of Splodgenessabounds in standard issue punk leopard print jeans
Centre: Debbie Harry of Blondie from 'Denis' single
Top right: Captain Sensible impersonating a yeti
Bottom right: Marc Bolan in glam fur-print cat-suit

Top left: Prince as Tarzan
Above: Stephanie Mills in sophisticated leopard pattern beaded chiffon
Top right: Diana Ross, queen of the urban jungle
Right and far right: Post-punk leopard prints – hers from The Kooky Shop, 1983, his from Baxby Fashion House, 1981 – both advertised in NME

49

GLASSES

All of us who wear glasses will now pause to salute Buddy Holly who taught us not to be ashamed of our condition. Now that not only Holly but also John Lennon, Elton John, Hank Marvin, Elvis Costello, John Denver, etc. have entered pop history, younger readers may find it difficult to imagine the stigma which glasses once conferred, and the limited selection of styles once available. Glasses used to be OK for nutty professors but not for the handsome, sexy or glamourous. Holly was no Rock Hudson, but until he flew off into that fatal sunset he was someone with whom the girls in school would have been happy to go to the junior prom and to dance with, cheek to cheek. He wasn't a goof, a jerk or a nurd, yet he wore glasses. Since the time when Holly showed it could be done, wearing glasses has not only become acceptable but at times (eg. the late sixties granny/Lennon glasses period) almost *de rigueur* – to the extent that people with 20–20 vision wore plain lenses for effect.

Buddy Holly (right) and Roy Orbison (left) in amazingly similar glasses

Above: The world of The Shadows seen through Hank Marvin's glasses
Top centre: John Lennon on 'Walls and Bridges' wearing five pairs of 'Lennon' glasses
Top right: Tony Benyon illustration of Elton John for NME, 1976 which shows how important his spectacular specs were to his image
Right: Elvis Costello on 'This Years Model'
Far right: Ad for Jam and Lennon glasses from Mark Lord Promotions NME, 1983

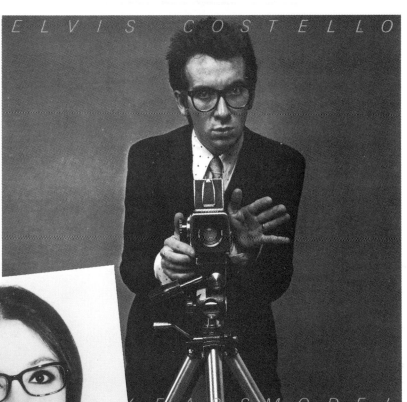

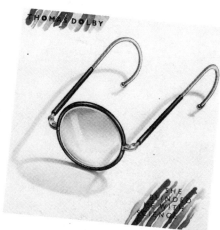

Bottom left: Nana Mouskouri, one of the very few female stars to have incorporated glasses into her image
Bottom right: Sleeve of Thomas Dolby's 'She Blinded Me With Science'

GLOVES

Originally a sign of class and elegance, gloves were rediscovered by Gene Vincent who found that leather bikers gloves could suit the spirit of rock and roll. One way or another, the pop star's hand clutching a microphone is a focus of our attention and a prime place for decoration. On stage gloves are scene dressing, not practical necessities, but lace or leather, sophisticated or studded, fingerless, worn on one hand only, long or short, there's a style to suit all types.

Top left: Gene Vincent on 'Dressed in Black'
Top right: Thin Lizzy in studded gloves
Above: Dave Vanian of The Damned on 'Love Song'
Left: Alvin Stardust in his 1970s black leather look
Right: Gina X on 'Nice Mover'

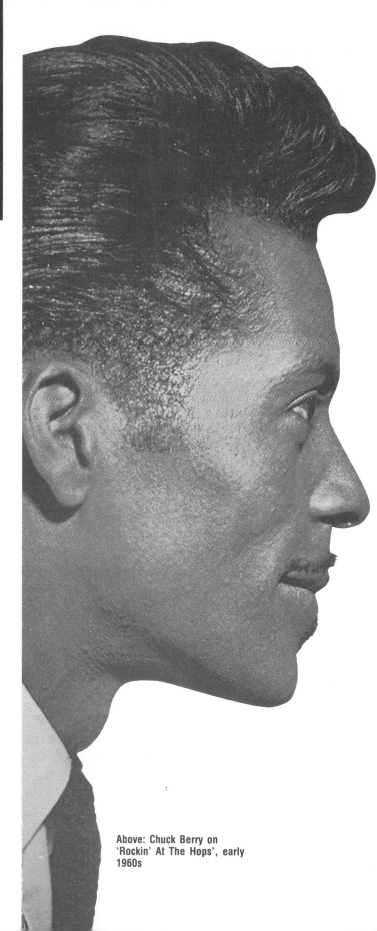

Above: Chuck Berry on 'Rockin' At The Hops', early 1960s

Short back n'sides

On the inside sleeve of the Stray Cats' first album there is a picture of the Nu Nile hair grease which they are famous not only for using but also for taking with them in bulk wherever they go. It is a touching tribute, a reminder that, at least in the early days of rock, popular music and hair grease were practically synonymous. Grease made the quiff possible in the same way that hair spray made possible the wondrous hair sculpture known as the beehive (see TEASED HAIR). But, unlike hair spray which is relatively new, liberally applied hair grease has always been a vital part of the pop scene – a big band jazz musician such as Bix Beiderbecke would have felt naked without the slicked-back hair which suggested gangsters in prohibition dives or black musicians in Harlem and Chicago. Beiderbecke may well have used Nu Nile although Black and White and Brylcream later became more popular. (Brylcream are even said to have sponsored a fifties Connie Francis record). Seventies punks preferred Vaseline or KY Jelly and punkabillies/psychobillies (a hybrid of punks and rockabillies) have carried on the sticky tradition with everything including soap and eggs. But the Popstyles 'Take it easy greasy' award must go to all those greasers (rockers) who, in the late fifties and early sixties, would use nothing on their hair but genuine axle grease.

Top: Early picture of Waylon Jennings, once Buddy Holly's base player (he gave up his seat on the fatal flight to The Big Bopper), now famous for his 'outlaw' Country music
Centre: Ian Hunter on 'Short Back 'n Sides', 1981
Above: German group Malaria! on 'New York Passage', 1982
Left: Bix Beiderbecke, jazz star of the 1920s, on 'Bix Beiderbecke and the Chicago Cornets'

GROUP IDENTITY

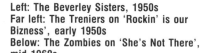

Left: The Beverley Sisters, 1950s
Far left: The Treniers on 'Rockin' is our Bizness', early 1950s
Below: The Zombies on 'She's Not There', mid 1960s
Bottom left: 'Fasten your wigs and gear down your moving parts. You, my groovy little souls, are about to go into orbit . . . and like with no rocket . . . just the fabulous OLYMPICS', 1961
Bottom right: The Supremes, early 1960s
Opposite page:
Main picture: The Temptations and Diana Ross and The Supremes, 1969
Top right: The Four Tops, mid 1960s
Centre right: ABC, 1982
Bottom right: Dream Express, late 1970s

Think of the Beatles around 1962–63 in identical collarless suits and then in 1969 on 'Abbey Road' all in different styles. What happened in between was the cult of the individual. Previously – for as long as pop music had existed – a band was a team machine. Rock inherited this structure, and in Doo-wop and Motown perfected the synchronization of music, movement and visual style. There might or might not be a lead singer who, like the band leader, would stand stylistically alone but the backing groups – the Pips, Vandellas, Miracles, etc. – exhibited an almost android-like suppression of the ego. But

the late sixties, obsessed with people doing their own thing, spelled doom for this unity of style. It's hard to know whether the actions of groups such as the Beatles in projecting separate identities for each member of the band reflected or created this ideology of the ego which would make the seventies, in Tom Wolfe's phrase, the 'Me Decade'.

Today we find that although they are not usually identical, many bands have a central visual theme which is expressed slightly differently by each member eg. Bananarama (see LUMBERJACK SHIRTS), Duran Duran (see UNIFORMS), Tik and Tok (see OTT), etc.

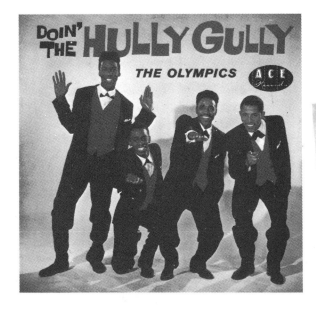

Clockwise from above:
Devo, late 1970s
The Jets on '100% Cotton',
1982
'The Ramones', 1976
The Residents whose true
identities remain hidden
behind their matching
eyeballs, 1982
Doo-wop revival group The
Darts, late 1970s

Hats are an astonishingly pervasive pop style, considering that they are generally associated with the older generation. But when pop stars are photographed or filmed it's most often just their faces which we see and hats have been used in their thousands as a shorthand to communicate the message appropriate to each of those faces. There is a hat to suit any star or mood and each is as valuable as a symbol as it is for keeping the rain off.

Left: George Melly in his classic Fedora
Above left: Bing Crosby in a Tyrolean style hat with feather
Above: Fats Waller in a bowler
Top left: Kenny Ball and his Jazzmen in Cossack-style hats for 'Midnight in Moscow', 1961
Top right: Slade – Dave Hill in top hat, Noddy Holder in wide brimmed felt hat, 1983
Right: James Brown in straw Stetson, 1981

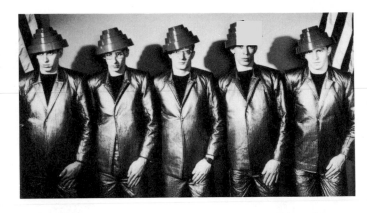

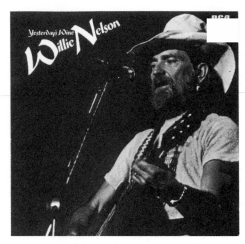

Top row from left:
April Love with giant sombrero
Willie Nelson on 'Yesterday's Wine' in crumpled straw hat
Devo in matching 'flowerpot' hats
Centre row from left:
John Denver with leather Stetson
Jimi Hendrix in black felt hat
Elton John in a straw boater
Left: Bob Marley and The Wailers in various Rasta hats and caps on 'Uprising'
Right: Madness logo with Mod hat from 'My Girl'

Village People 'Go West' wearing hard hat, Stetson, motor cycle helmet, sailor hat, Brando cap and Indian feather headress

HATS for MODS

FABULOUS FOR STYLE.
QUALITY, COMFORT
& VALUE

69/6

Send now for this hat, the very latest offer from Modique. High Crown, high ribbon & ½ braided brim puts you way out ahead. This is a hand finished product with leather interior band, smart lining, and is fully waterproofed. Don't miss this offer! Avoid disappointment! Use the coupon below to ORDER NOW!!

COLOURS MIDNIGHT BLUE, DONKEY BROWN SLATE GREY

SEND **69/6** TO: MODIQUE · 44 STATION LANE · HORNCHURCH · ESSEX

Sheena Easton (top left), David Bowie (top centre) and John Taylor of Duran Duran (bottom right) demonstrate different ways of looking good in a trilby
Left: Michael Grant of Musical Youth in bowler and braces
Top right: Malcolm McLaren wearing a Worlds End felt hat
Centre: 'The very latest offer from Modique. High crown, high ribbon – ½" braided brim puts you way out ahead.' ad from DISC, 1964

With patterns produced by printing instead of weaving, the classic Hawaiian shirt shouts rather than whispers its exotic origins. Logically these garments could be considered under the ETHNIC heading but their continuing popularity nudges them into a class of their own.

Right: Elvis Presley on the soundtrack album of 'Blue Hawaii', 1970
Below: Gove Scrivenor dressed for the beach on 'Coconut Gove', 1979
Bottom: The Dead Sea Surfers on 'Don't Sing Aloha . . . When I Goha', 1983

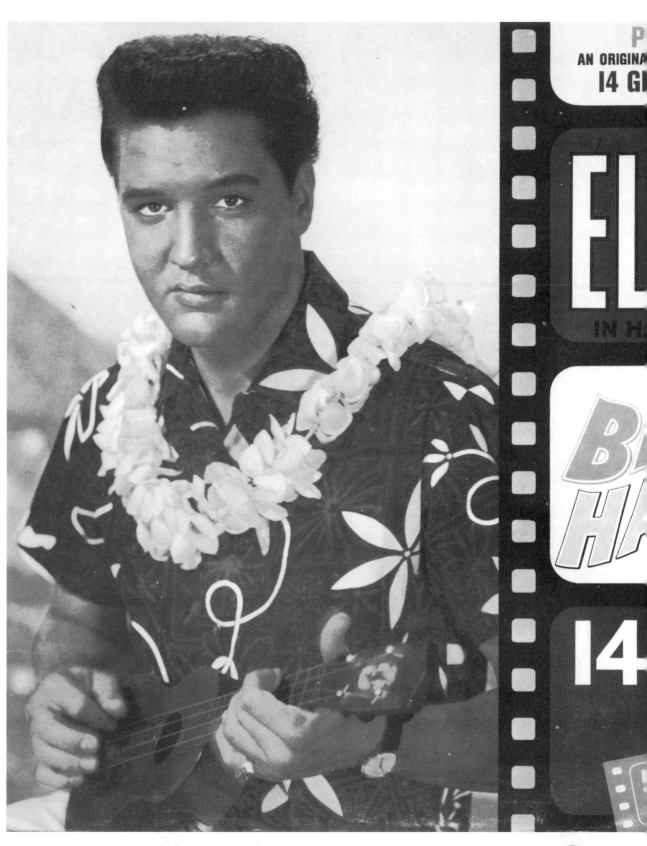

HEADBANDS

The advent of really long hair in the late sixties created a need for something to keep it in place and out of the musician's eyes. At the same time the prevailing hippy mentality brought an appreciation of all things ethnic. Suddenly Indians, not cowboys, were the heroes and thus the headband came into its own. A decade later, disco revived the headband as a form of jewellery and around the same time some post-punks began experimenting with growing their hair longer and keeping it in place with a cloth headband. Finally in the eighties with the cult of the athletic, the sweatband made an appearance (see Olivia Newton-John in SPORTSWEAR). For those into heavy metal, however, time has stood still; hair is as long as ever and the headband hangs on.

Right: Randy California of Spirit in hippy-style headband
Top right: Celena Duncan with the kind of thin headband which became fashionable in the late 1970s
Centre right: Dealer in American Indian-style outfits complete with headbands
Bottom left: Jack Casady of Hot Tuna (ex Jefferson Airplane) in hippy headband
Bottom centre: Debbie Harry on 'Koo Koo'
Bottom right: Flower power headband on Electric Banana's 'The Sixties'

Musicians may popularize certain styles of jewellery but its most important pop styles function has been as a medium for fans to advertise their allegiances. Unfortunately you can no longer send off for these items, but if you compare the jewellery you could have had in 1957 and 1973 only the stars' names have changed. Today the need to keep your idols close to you lives on but fans tend to wear the same styles as their idol rather than a photo.

THE BEATLES

Get with it! wear a **BEAT BEETLE** FOB BROOCH

BEATLE FANS wear this Fabulous Antique Gilded Brooch and ensure your idols remain at the Top of the Charts

Send P.O. for **2/11d.** NOW !
(INCLUDING postage and packing)

GENUINE OFFER — AVAILABLE FROM

ETIQUETTE FASHIONS LTD.
METROPOLE WORKS, WALTHAM ABBEY, ESSEX

EXCLUSIVE 16×12

THE PHOTO BANGLE
(Not illustrated)
The Rage of Hollywood !
Made of lightweight metal with beautiful untarnishable gold finish containing 9 different pictures of your favourite singing stars.
7/6 inc. P. & P.

The 6-Star Identity Bracelet, (Not illustrated) contains 6 photos of your favourite stars. Gold finish untarnishable link chain **5/-** each, inc. post & packing
Your initials or name stylishly engraved on any article add **2/-** extra

THE GUITAR BROOCH
All-metal with beautiful untarnishable gold finish, with Blue, Red or Green filigree safety catch pin fastening with back that opens and contains 11 different photos of your favourite stars, or you can insert your own personal photo.
4/6 inc. P. & P.

SHIRT or BLOUSE CUFF LINKS. Latest American fastening, with large 1" deep coloured photo of T.S. or ELVIS PRESLEY (only) **10/6** per pair inc. p. & p.

THE 8-STAR BALL BRACELET.
Beautiful Gold finish, untarnishable link chain with four transparent globes, each globe contains 2 photos of your favourite male singing stars.

★ **SEND YOUR ORDER NOW** —
These novelties make ideal Xmas gifts—so order one for your friend at the same time.
(TRADE ENQUIRIES INVITED)

The 8-star Ball Bracelet is the rage of the U.S.A. this fall. A wonderful piece of costume jewellery with a million dollar appearance.
8-STAR BALL BRACELET SENT POST PAID 7/6 each

THE HOLLYWOOD NOVELTY CO., 8 ARGYLL STREET, LONDON, W.1

Or write for FREE mail order list.

Beat boys and girls go for BEETLE JEWELLERY

Everyone's wearing the black beetle motif—on this lovely bracelet (12/6), or up-to-the-minute cuff links (15/-). Also available on ear clips (10/6), pendant on chain (7/6), brooch ring (10/6), adjustable (8/6). All jewellery 22 ct. gold plated and untarnishable.

Prices include postage and packing

Go for BEETLE JEWELLERY

AVAILABLE ONLY FROM

PRELUDE JEWELLERY LTD.
70 ST. JOHN STREET, LONDON, E.C.1

and recording with Tomorrow. Keith writes all the group's stage ... Through a ...

JUST ARRIVED ! San Francisco Hippy Jewellery ! The Polytrend Collection of Beautiful Jewellery for Beautiful People !

HIPPY EARRINGS
Hippy Earrings Gold finish flower rosette ear clip, creole shape with gently tinkling 18 ct. gold plate bells
ONLY **15/6** PAIR

IT'S HERE HIPPY RING
Hippy Ring. Beautifully moulded 22 ct. gold plate adjustable band with 2 gently tinkling 18 ct. gold plate bells.
ONLY **15/-**

HIPPY BRACELET
Hippy Bracelet/Anklet 22 ct. gold plate adjustable chain with 5 gently tinkling 18 ct. gold plate bells. Can also be worn as a belt.
ONLY **17/6**

HIPPY NECKLACE
Hippy Necklace Gold finish chain with 22 ct. gold plate flower motif medallion and 3 gently tinkling 18 ct. gold plate bells. Can also be worn as a necklace.
ONLY **20/-**

HIPPY BELT
Hippy Belt Gold finish adjustable chain and centre disc with 5 gently tinkling 18 ct. gold plate bells. Can also be worn as a necklace.
ONLY **23/6**

COMPLETE HIPPY SET 82/6
ALL POST PAID

POLYTREND LTD.,
23 Gt. Titchfield Street, London, W.1
(Dept. NME/95)
Trade Enquiries Invited

BERLYN ARCADE

Silver **ARROW** (or Gold)
Silver £3.75 9CT £13.95

ALL PRICES INCLUDE AN 18" STERLING SILVER OR 9 CT GOLD CHAIN

AT THAT PRICE YOU CAN AFFORD A QUIVER !

Solid Silver **SCREW**
£5.75 or have it in Gold £29.50

SHARP PRICE **BLADE**
Silver £4.25, 9CT £27.95

WISHBONE
Silver £5.75, 9CT £30.75

FOR YOUNG CHICS AND RANDY ROOSTERS

A-Z INITIALS ANY TYPE OF LETTERS A-Z Silv £3.45 9CT £19.75

ALL OUR GOODS SOLID SILVER OR 9 CARAT GOLD
QUOTE YOUR ACCESS No OR MAKE P.O. OR CHEQUE PAYABLE TO:

GARY BERLYN
Dept NME, 32 Market Row Arcade, London SW9 9DL
7 DAY MONEY BACK GUARANTEE SUBJECT TO HANDLING CHARGE

ONLY **£9.20**
Available only from
SPECIAL INTRODUCTORY OFFER

FINE ART DESIGN
the ORIGINAL **HIS-N-HERS BULLET PENDANT**
REAL .38 Calibre Police Special bullet in beautiful silver finish, mounted on a 24" solid silver chain only **£9.20**

Also available - **NICKEL JACKETED BULLET** with matching chain only **£3.80**

or mounted on a key ring with a beautiful black leather fob only **£3.20**

ORIGINAL GIFTS FOR THAT SPECIAL PEBSON (All prices include p. + p.)
Trade enquiries welcome.
Send cheque or P.O. NOW to Dept. NME Fine Art Design, P.O. Box 15, Broken-Gate Lane, Denham, Uxbridge, Middx UB9 HLA. Dispatch by return — money back if not absolutely delighted.

Top left: Beetle fob brooch from Etiquette Fashions Ltd. NME, 1963
Top right: Guitar brooch which opens to reveal '11 different photos of your favourite stars' and cufflinks with 'coloured photo of T.S. (Tommy Steele) or Elvis Presley' from The Hollywood Novelty Co. ad in NME, 1957
Above: 'His-n-hers bullet pendant' from Fine Art Design NME, 1979
Left: Razor blade and other jewellery from Gary Berlyn NME, 1976
Bottom left: 'San Francisco Hippy Jewellery . . . for Beautiful People !' with 'gently tinkling bells' from Polytrend Ltd. NME, 1967
Centre left: Beetle baubles from Prelude Jewellery Ltd. NME, 1963
Right: 'Star album' and 'Gilt framed scroll necklace' with photos of Donny Osmond, Dave Cassidy, Marc Bolan, Gary Glitter from J. Powell ad in NME, 1973

SEE THIS !

INITIALLED SIGNET RINGS
for Ladies or Gents, only **35p**

STAINLESS STEEL ZODIAC MEDALLION
with 26 in. Chain Star sign, only **60p**

POP STAR BOOK KEY RING
In leather with 11 pop photos, only **30p**

FRINGED SATIN SCARVES
(50 in. x 5 in.) Dave, Donny, Marc, Elvis, Bowie, Slade and Gary Glitter **60p**

STAR ALBUM

GILT FRAMED SCROLL NECKLACE
Chain, Photo of Donny Osmond, Dave Cassidy, Marc Bolan, Gary Glitter, only **30p**

All sent post free (U.K. only)
J. POWELL (NME), 20 EDITH AVENUE, PEACEHAVEN, SUSSEX

PERSONALISE

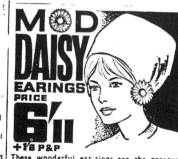

Top left: Photo ID jewellery from S. & R. Kiosks
Ltd. NME, 1957. Choose from Pat Boone, Johnnie
Ray, Liberace, Dickie Valentine, Frankie Laine,
etc.
Bottom left: Diamante necklace set from the
glamourous days before rock 'n roll rebellion, ad
for Barbican Supplies in NME, 1954
Bottom centre: 'Get the gear today from: M. & B.
Supplies' – linen Mod daisy earings NME, 1965
Centre row from top:
'Top of the "EAR RING HIT PARADE" ', bugle and
drummer earings from Star Productions NME,
1955
'Put excitement into your life with our gold
coloured foam rubber lined bra – sticks on and
stays on until you want to remove it. Be a "WOW"
at your next party, a knock-out under see-thro
clothes.' ad from West Midlands Distributors
(B'ham) Ltd. NME, 1969
'Real horn' pendants from Shegren Ltd. NME, 1975
Bob Dylan belt buckle, J. N. Souvenirs NME, 1978
Above from top:
Elvis pendant from Jeremy St. James NME, 1977
Heavy metal logo pendants, Blaze SOUNDS, 1982
TOTP pendant, Pop World Enterprises NME, 1975

JUMPSUITS

Evolving from such diverse influences as Winston Churchill's siren suit, flying suits and industrial overalls, jumpsuits in the pop world come in two basic types: the *catsuit* is tight and slinky, usually made of a stretchy fabric which allows it to cling to the body like a second skin. The *boilersuit*, on the other hand, is loose fitting with more practical connotations.

What these sub-types have in common is that they are both one-piece garments and allow the stage performer freedom to move around without his/her clothes slipping into disarray. Jumpsuits were particularly popular in the glam rock era and among the more physically active pop stars.

Clockwise from above:
Space oddity David Bowie, 1973
A very different style of jumpsuit worn by Rod Stewart in 1980
Rick James in chest-revealing rhinestone-studded jumpsuit, 1982
Country-pop singer Tanya Tucker in skin-tight red jumpsuit on 'TNT', 1978

Leather is a must for any rock and roll animal. No matter how refined, the implication of the beast is always there; civilization and time roll back to reveal the scent and feel of the jungle. Studded, zipped, rough or smooth, leather conjours up not only the animal but also the hunter/killer. Thus the pop star in tight black leather trousers stalks the stage like his or her most ancient of ancestors. To hell with civilization, this is rock and roll.

The most typical use of leather in the pop world is in the motorbike jacket. Not only do performers wear them but fans, especially of punk bands, inscribe the name of their favourite group on the back using paint, studs, etc. This mark of allegiance is – given the cost of a motorbike jacket and the time needed to wear it in properly – just this side of tattooing in its degree of dedication.

Top left: Marianne Faithfull in leather, for which she was famous
Top: Girlschool 'Hit And Run' in black leather jackets and jeans
Centre left: Close fitting leather skirts from The Kooky Shop NME, 1983
Centre right: Leather jeans from Sharon Kidson NME, 1979
Bottom left: Infa Riot in leather bike jackets
Bottom right: Heaven in leather jackets and jeans

Above: Alice Cooper in leather top with under-the-crotch strap and thigh-high boots over ripped jumpsuit, early 1970s

Top centre: Sleeve of 'The Secret Life Of Punks' compilation shows the use of leather motor cycle jackets as portable billboards for advertising musical tastes

Right: Beki Bondage (ex-Vice Squad) in leather skirt, belts and wristbands with fashion accessory whip

Clockwise from top:
Freddie Mercury of Queen
Steve Strange of Visage
Julian Cope of the Teardrop Explodes
Fashion
Motor bike jackets from Stormglade
NME, 1981

Sizes: Guys 34/44, Girls 8/16. Real hide motorbike jackets, all black £41.95. Real hide motor bike jackets, black and white £41.95. Black Leather Waistcoat £9.95.

JACKETS

TROUSERS

Bondage (plenty of zips & D-Rings) black, white, mid-blue, red £12.75. leopard leggings £8.95. tartan (zips & d-rings) £10.95. bum flaps tartan, leopard or ocelot print + plain colours as Bondage Trousers £1.60

(DEPT X)

STORMGLADE
1 CRANBOURNE
ALLEY, LEICESTER
SQUARE, LONDON WC2.

LINGERIE

Fashion historians have noted how many garments progress from underwear to accepted outerwear. Pop music's contribution has included Annabella Lwin of Bow Wow Wow demonstrating Vivienne Westwood's idea of wearing bras over t-shirts, but the idea didn't catch on in a big way. More typical is the straightforward selling of female pop musicians as sex symbols by showing them in suggestive garments from Victorian cami-knickers to filmy lingerie. But, in contrast to the sexist hype, many female pop stars have utilized lingerie as a shock tactic, overthrowing conventions of dress as a sign of their own daring.

Top left: Bliss in see-through baby doll
Top right: Tanya Tucker on 'Should I Do It' in camiknickers and corset – a striking change of image from her JUMPSUIT
Above left: Kim Goody in a Victorian nightdress on 'Wait in Line'
Above right: Max of The Weekend Swingers in Jerry Lee Lewis knickers
Centre: Camidress 'trimmed with thrilling frilling' from Joy Claydon ad in NME, 1973 – 'Tops at no. 1 Smash hit for discos & parties'
Right: 'Super for dance or beach' Baby Doll from Kendale Ltd. ad in NME, 1968
Far right: Sarah Dash (ex-Labelle) in a strapless corset

It is ironic that classical music used to be referred to as 'long hair music'. But with the original rockers' QUIFFS, the Beatles' 'lovable mop tops', the Stones' decadent collar-length locks, the Ronettes' or Mari Wilson's beehives (see TEASED HAIR), the shoulder length shag of hippy and heavy metal groups or even some punks' gravity-defying mohicans (see SHAVED HEADS), rock music seems to have a stronger claim to the title of 'long hair music'. Americans can remember the billboards and bumper stickers which pleaded 'Make America Beautiful Get A Haircut'. Common sense should have told them that, given time, even dangerous subversives such as John Lennon would get a haircut. But in the strange world of heavy metal – The Land That Time Forgot – time does somehow stand still. Even today in the personal columns of music papers like *Sounds* the great majority of want-ads placed by girls seeking boys demand long hair.

This page:
Left: Sweet with typical 1970s glam hair styles
Bottom left: John Mayall, the late 1960s hippy look personified
Below: 'Dad, dig this new mad fad. It's a gas! Now you can don a Beatle cut quick as a flash . . . Choose Jet Black or Liverpool Brown and she'll love you. Swing, man, Swing!' Beat wig from Montrose Products ad in DISC, 1963. 'Liverpool Brown'?
Below right: Home hair straightener kit from Yvette Hair Care Products ad in NME, 1974
Opposite page:
Main picture: Heavy metal pin-up John Sykes (ex-Thin Lizzy) of Whitesnake
Bottom right: Another Whitesnake hero, David Coverdale
Top right: Harvey Bainbridge of Hawkwind

THE WORLD OF JOHN MAYALL Vol. 2

checkin' up on my baby
broken wings
my time after awhile
ready to ride
double crossin' time
leaping christine
killing time
brand new start
2401
someday after awhile
(you'll be sorry)
she's too young
I can't quit you baby

DECCA

LUMBERJACK SHIRTS

They're sensible and basic and earthy and butch (even worn by the Bananarama girls). They bring a whiff of the country to the most urban pop star. Get one and go chop down a tree.

Top left: Kenny Rogers
Above: Big Country
Right: Bananarama

LUREX AND LAME

Lurex is a knitted fabric which includes metallic threads. Lame is a woven material in which metallic threads produce a solid shiny surface. Between them they can make a musician sparkle and shine and literally look like a star (especially if stage lighting uses these fabrics to advantage). This combination has proved such a success that the gold lame suit has become *the* definitive uniform of pop. A tradition in its own right, it has passed from generation to generation – a modern equivalent of the matador's suit of lights.

Top: Martha and the Vandellas looking lovely in lurex, mid 1960s
Three versions of the irrepressible lame jacket, pop's classic garment –
Far left: Ace Cannon, early 1960s
Centre left: Gary Glitter, mid 1970s
Near left: Martin Fry of ABC, 1982

Shrink

AMSP 7468

Silver Genes It Shows Con Dition
Energy DuDu Duwa Ships
Photos by Anska Nalki
Produced by Modern Leopard for

On air Tributes and Music

THE KING
IS DEAD...

THE NIGHT ELVIS DIED 16th AUGUST 1977

DECCA

THE
WORLD
OF
BILLY
FURY

halfway to paradise
because of love
in summer
nobody's child
a thousand stars
magic eyes
I'd never find another you
last night was made for love
like I've never been gone
once upon a dream
push push
letter full of tears

LITTLE RICHARD
Whole Lotta Shakin'

Top left: Shrink, 1979
Centre left: *The* man, *the* pose,
the suit – Elvis in the late 1950s
(Unfortunately his taste in suits
went downhill from here – see
RHINESTONES)
Bottom left: Little Richard late in
his career
Top right: Many followed in Elvis's
footsteps and in his suit – Billy
Fury, early 1960s
Left: Sandie Shaw in the mid
1960s makes a little lurex go a
long way on 'The Sandie Shaw
Supplement'

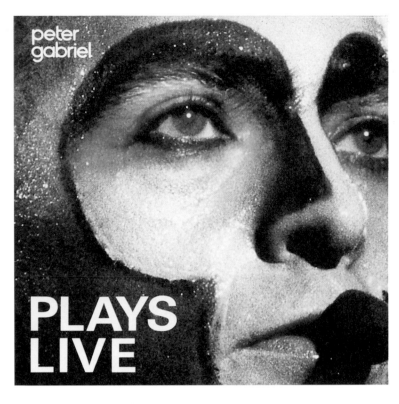

peter
gabriel

PLAYS LIVE

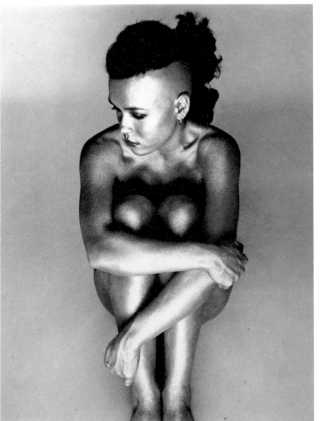

Above: Peter Gabriel, 1983
Right: Bowie as Aladin
Sane, 1973
Below: Baccara – Spanish
psychedellia, 1978
Left: Annabella Lwin of Bow
Wow Wow, early 1980s

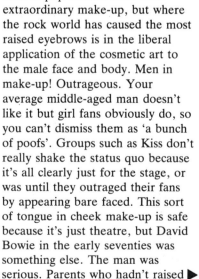

Lots of pop women have worn extraordinary make-up, but where the rock world has caused the most raised eyebrows is in the liberal application of the cosmetic art to the male face and body. Men in make-up! Outrageous. Your average middle-aged man doesn't like it but girl fans obviously do, so you can't dismiss them as 'a bunch of poofs'. Groups such as Kiss don't really shake the status quo because it's all clearly just for the stage, or was until they outraged their fans by appearing bare faced. This sort of tongue in cheek make-up is safe because it's just theatre, but David Bowie in the early seventies was something else. The man was serious. Parents who hadn't raised ▶

75

their sons to wear lipstick, pan-cake and eye shadow, or their daughters to fancy such abominations were scared. But today even Bowie is not obviously made-up and few of today's teenagers or those ex-teens who worshipped Bowie walk the streets in facial drag. Yet Bowie did provide an enduring model which any male can always relate to as part of a less restricted definition of being a man. For those who feel hemmed in by our society's narrow definition of masculinity, Bowie's Aladin Sane and Ziggy Stardust are there to provide an alternative. Others have had an influence, of course. (Jagger in *Performance*, Arthur Brown, Roy Wood, etc). The tradition continues, but Bowie's gender bending make-up will never be equalled for its daring, simply because his were the first serious experiments with pop androgony.

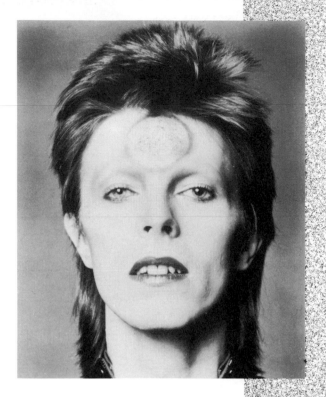

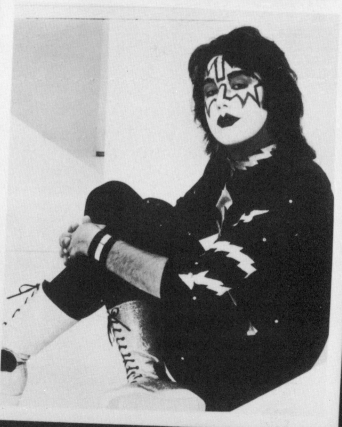

Opposite page:
Top right: Male make-up pioneer Arthur Brown without his flaming headress, 1968
Top left: David Bowie in 1973
Bottom left: Lou Reed in black lipstick, eyeliner and nail varnish, 1972
Bottom centre: Fish of Marillion, 1983
Bottom right: Dee Snider of Twisted Sister epitomising the charm of heavy metal, 1983

This page:
Above: One of Malcolm McLaren's Buffalo Gals, 1983
Right: Kiss prior to their unmasking in 1980. Throughout the 1970s their make-up was such an essential part of their act that they wisely refused to be photographed or interviewed bare faced

Top left: Boy George, 1983
Above right: Toyah from
'Brave New World' picture
disc, 1982
Left: David Sylvian, 1980

78

Above: Steve Strange of Visage, 1982
Far right: Monkey of The Adicts, 1982
Right: Adam Ant, 1981

Watching old film clips of pop singers such as Sandie Shaw, Cilla Black, Lulu or Nancy Sinatra, one is surprised by the fact that, compared with today, the earliest mini skirts weren't really very short. All that shock horror sensation was over just a few inches of thigh. Today's pop ladies, especially punk types such as Beki Bondage and Wendy O. Williams, have taken the mini to heights above which further escalation would render the garment rather pointless. Minis are especially interesting because, like collarless SUITS and fashion BOOTS for women, they are exceptions to the rule of pop styles leading the way for mainstream fashion. But would even Mary Quant have had as much impact on the world without those singers and dancers who showed her creations to a wider public via TV pop shows such as 'Ready, Steady, Go'?

Left: Charlie Dore on
'Listen', 1981
Above: The Jodelles, 1983
Right: 'It's No. 1 in the Carnaby Street
hit parade' Modern Gear of Carnaby
Street ad from NME, 1966

IT'S No.1 IN THE CARNABY STREET HIT PARADE!!

THIS mini SKIRT

FOR PRICE—ONLY 24s. PP 2s. 6d.
FOR STYLE—SIMPLICITY CUT.
FOR VALUE—HARD WEARING.
QUALITY, WOOL MELTON.
FOR COLOUR—DEEP PURPLE, FASH
BLACK, or LAMB GREY (state ch
Hip sizes 32, 34, 36, 38.
SPECIAL OFFER!
Fully fashion-shaped belt, black, large
type buckle 3s. 6d.

READY STEADY GO

BLACK

IMAGINATION
IN THE HEAT OF THE NIGHT

Above left: Modette suit
from **Individual Trading
Co**. RECORD MIRROR, 1980
Above: Sharon Kidson ad
from NME, 1981
Right: Minis 'In The Heat
of The Night', 1982
Bottom right: Jennie
McKeown of the
Bellestars, 1980

Above: Cilla Black on TV, mid 1960s
Below: 1967 NME ad from
Granny's Emporium –
note that despite the
drawing the skirt is
described as being
'2″ above knee'
Right: Toni Basil
in a ra-ra skirt.
She helped
to make them
fashionable

No Stone Unturned
THE ROLLING STONES

Stereo—The tracks marked *
are mono recordings
electronically reprocessed to
give stereo effect on
stereo equipment.

WHAT YOU WAITIN' FOR

STARGARD

Perhaps the only really consistent aspect of pop styles is their inclination to go Over The Top. Although the fans don't usually take things as far, the extremes seen on stages, record covers and press photos do have the effect of encouraging an expansion of what is deemed acceptable. Where will it end? One suggestion is found in the performance of Jordan (once manager and singer with Adam and the Ants) in Derek Jarman's film *Jubilee*. In this cinematic vision of a future Britain where pop barons rule the world, the likes of Jordan can – at least for a few minutes – rule the airwaves as Britannia in stockings, suspender belt and see-through knickers. Today things are (a bit) more restrained on T.V. pop shows, but on stage pretty much anything goes – except in middle America where Wendy O. Williams was actually arrested for indecent behaviour. Generally, however, most pop people go for extravagance rather than indecency.

Opposite top left: Tik and Tok 'Summer in the City', 1982
Bottom left: Gong, 1971
Bottom right: Stargard, 1978
Top right: Rolling Stones 'No Stone Unturned', 1973
This page left: Rick James, 1982
Top: Techno Twins, 1983

Left: Jordan as Britannia, an instant pop star in Derek Jarman's film 'Jubilee'. Perhaps the original punk when manageress of McLaren/Westwood's Sex boutique and singer/manager with Adam and the Ants, Jordan was as outrageous and OTT in real life as Britannia was in the film.
Above: The Plasmatics on 'Coup d'État' looking as sweet and subtle as usual, 1982
Below: All American group the Sic F*cks work hard to shock but the end product is more fun fancy dress than subversive

PARKAS

Like DRAPES, the PARKA's popularity owed more to the fans than the stars. A longish type of anorak or wind-cheater, its origins are as a military version of the Eskimos' skin coat. Warm, practical and cheap, it fitted the needs of Britain's mods who rode scooters. For the pop performer, however, who would usually travel by car rather than be exposed to the elements and who could afford something smarter, slicker and more experimental, the parka usually stayed in the closet. During the mod revival of the seventies, the parka was rediscovered and one group even called themselves 'The Merton Parkas' but it should be pointed out that on their album sleeve they appear dressed in mod suits.

Clockwise from top left:
Publicity still for the film 'Quadrophenia' – an affectionate tribute by the Who to their original mod fans. The Who's faces can be seen in the scooter's mirrors. Peter Quaife, original bass player with the Kinks, in a rare picture of a mod musician actually wearing a parka, mid 1960s
Ad from NME, 1965
Ad from NME, 1979
Ad from SOUNDS, 1980

85

PEROXIDE

At one time bleached hair was the sort of thing that pop people e.g. Heinz like everyone else tried to keep secret. It wasn't really until punk arrived, spitting in the eye of the respectable and the natural, that the peroxide bottle came out of the bathroom cupboard. In Britain it led to CRAZY COLOUR (which works best on bleached hair) while in the US it found a definitive exponent in Debbie Harry. Signifying both artifice and – probably via a heritage of film stars such as Jean Harlow and Marilyn Monroe – a raw sexiness, a good-times mentality, even a deliberate tackiness, peroxide is a punk antithesis of what hippy values had come to imply in the seventies. Peroxide's artificial quality has also been used by electronic persons such as Gary Numan to denote the musician as android/alien.

But all of this is very recent history and special credit must go to the likes of Dolly Parton who dared to flaunt artifice – not even the hair itself is real, it's a wig – before punks were out of the original safety-pins holding up their nappies. True style never has to hide behind notions of 'good taste'.

Left: Dolly Parton 'Heart-break Express', 1982
Above: Debbie Harry 'Island of Lost Souls' picture disc, 1982
Right: Vince Neil of Mötley Crüe, 1983

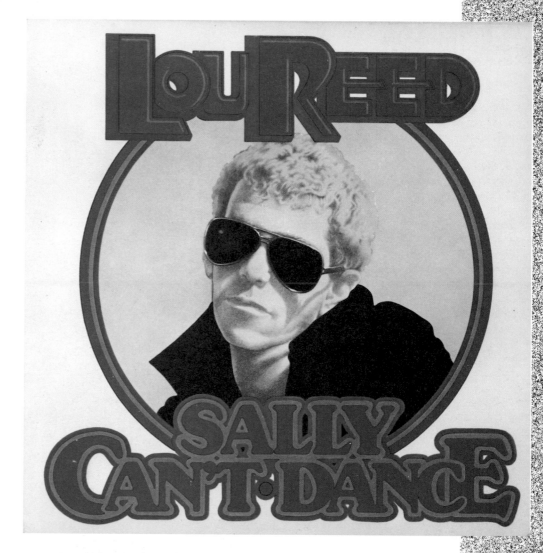

Far left: Bette Bright
'Rhythm Breaks the
Ice', 1981
Above: Lou Reed, 1974
Left: Gary Numan of
Tubeway Army, 1979

Known in the US as braids, plaits are a traditional way of tidying and decorating hair used by many societies from red Indians to middle European peasants. In the seventies there was a surge of interest in African culture and hair styles knotted into lots of tiny plaits caught on first among blacks and then among those whites who look to blacks for stylistic inspiration. These tiny plaits are often threaded with little beads to produce a sort of head jewellery which in movement has the effect of fringing. While not inventing plaits pop musicians have long made use of them. One of the initial inspirations for this book was seeing a Lene Lovich concert in the late seventies at which almost all of a huge audience of girl fans wore large plaits like Lene's.

Right: Lene Lovich displays the plaits which are her trademark, 1979
Bottom left: Sheila Chandra of Monsoon uses her plait as part of a traditional Indian image
Left: George Clinton displays his tightly knotted African style plaiting complete with beads and feathers
Top left: Stevie Wonder on 'Hotter Than July' sporting a full head of beads
Top right: Syreeta on the cover of 'One To One' with a multitude of tightly knotted plaits

In the hippy era the word plastic became the most severe of all forms of abuse. Not only objects but also people were referred to as plastic if they were thought to be insincere. But that time was both preceded and followed by the two great ages of plastic. Firstly, in the mid-sixties there was Swinging London which saw plastic as the material of the future with vinyl boots and macs and mini dresses with clear acetate windows. This delightful excess of artifice caused the pro-nature reaction led by the hippies, which in turn produced the glam and the anti-nature, pro-plastic punk eras. Each teenage generation has to define itself as different from the last and the plastic versus organic dichtomy has been an excellent tool in this process.

WET LOOK
ULTRA GLOSSY WETTEST of WET-LOOK DRESS AND DANCEWEAR in SPRAY-ON FIT SPECIALLY COATED BLACK LYCRA

MINI-DRESS ILLUS £13·50
MINI-SKIRT £7·50
DRAIN PIPES £14·50
CATSUIT ILLUS £17·50

ANY SIZE SUPERFAST DELIVERY PP 75p

DANCERS PARTYGOERS MODELS

She~an~me of London
FUN FASHION
Stiletto Boots & Shoes readily available

Exciting and Unusual
Erotic garments of all kinds —
Extra shiny Plastic Fantastic —
Soft stretchy super sheen
Leather Look

Top left: Siouxsie Sioux (without the Banshees) in an outfit designed for maximum shock value performing at one of her first gigs in 1976
Top right: Ad for The Kooky Shop SOUNDS 1983
Bottom right: Virna Lindt in 1960s pose, 1983
Right: 1982 NME ad for Siouxsie's PVC supplier
Above: German group the Cruisers, late 1970s

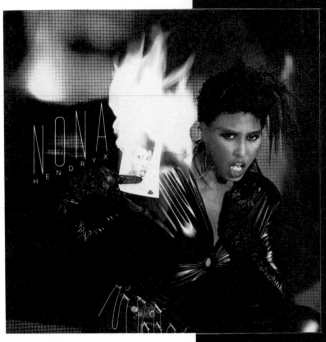

Above: Nona Hendryx
(ex-Labelle), 1983
Right: Dale Bozzio of Missing Persons
carries on in the early 1980s where
Barbarella left off
Below: Toto Coelo in a colourful
parody of punk plastic bin
liners, 1982

Originally referring to the visual effect of mind-altering drugs, 'psychedelic' came to refer to a style of dress, make-up and graphics which pop stars and fans revelled in during the late sixties. These clothes challenged established ideas of good taste but the roots of pyschedelic designs with their bright colours and swirling patterns can be traced back to the paisley patterns which came from the Orient. The style was revived briefly in Britain in the late seventies and early eighties by bands such as Scarlet Party and Mood Six and then passed back, for the time being, into oblivion.

FOR ELEGIBLE TRENDSETTERS ONLY

Stay "way in" with this fabulous crease resistant spun rayon dress. In three flamboyant flower designed colours. Pink, Green and Blue. Complete with zingy pleated cuffs. Approximately 3in. above knee. Sizes 34in., 36in., 38in. bust, and it's yours for only 79/6 p & p 3/6. Please state size required and second colour choice.

Send today for the exclusive offer. C:W.O. to:

Emma's Boutique, Dept. NME1, Terminal House, Station Road, Shepperton, Middlesex. *Personal Shoppers welcome*

79'6 POST & PACKING 3'6

NYLON TOP 25/- + P. & P. 3/6

CONTRAST BACKGROUND IN A BIG, MODERN PAISLEY PATTERN

Clockwise from above:
The Fool, who designed the Apple boutique and its clothes for the Beatles in 1967
Annabels Togs tempts the readers of NME in 1970 with a "machine washable nylon top . . . in a big, modern paisley pattern"
Earlier readers of NME could go psychedlic with Emma's Boutique in 1967
The Rolling Stones entered their psychedlic period with 'Their Satanic Majesties Request' in 1967
The Rumour carry on the tradition with 'Purity of Essence' in 1980

QUIFFS

To make a quiff, take a large handful of long hair from the back of the head, coat with plenty of grease, comb forward for one half the length of the hair and then reverse direction as quickly as possible. Comb back the hair over the ears and plaster down around the back of the head as close as you can to where you started. Then, using the fingers and palm (and a fine tooth comb if necessary), create a valley in the middle of the peak. Take care not to bump into things or let anyone get close to you – kissing, for example, should be done at a 45-degree angle. Renew with grease and comb at fifteen-minute intervals for the rest of your life.

As the alternative hairstyle of the late 1950s, the quiff inevitably became a symbol of rock 'n roll rebellion. By the early 1960s it was *the* style for American and British pop stars such as Bobby Rydell (above) and Billy Fury (opposite page top). Today Dave Taylor (opposite bottom left) and the British teddy boys stick to the traditional quiff while Brian Setzer of the Stray Cats (right) and Bal of the Sting-Rays (opposite bottom right) have both created new kinds of quiffs for the 1980s.

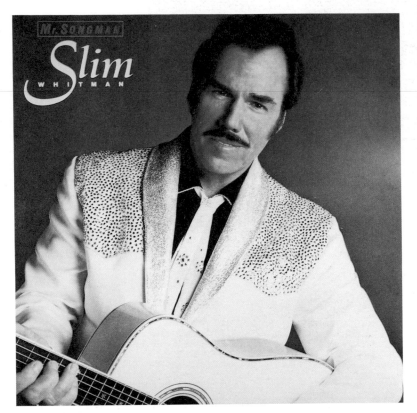

MR. SONGMAN
Slim
WHITMAN

Porter Wagoner
TODAY

EVERYTHING
IS EVERYTHING
Diana Ross

COME TOGETHER / (They Long To Be) CLOSE TO YOU
THE LONG AND WINDING ROAD / MY PLACE
I LOVE YOU (Call Me) / EVERYTHING IS EVERYTHING
HOW ABOUT YOU
DOOBEDOOD'NDOOBE, DOOBEDOOD'NDOOBE, DOOBEDOOD'NDOO
BABY IT'S LOVE / AIN'T NO SAD SONG
I'M STILL WAITING

Tamla
Motown

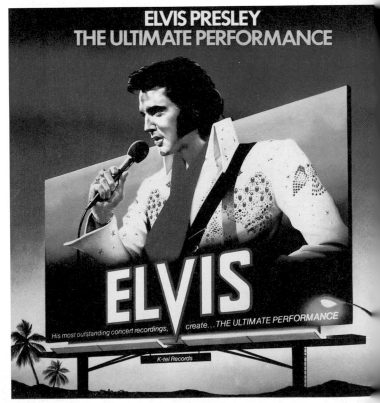

ELVIS PRESLEY
THE ULTIMATE PERFORMANCE

ELVIS

His most outstanding concert recordings, create...THE ULTIMATE PERFORMANCE

K-tel Records

First produced in Strasbourg, on the River Rhine, these fake diamonds of hardened paste have given the music business one of its finest weapons in the battle for our attention. Cheap, flashy and inviting excess, the rhinestone provided country musicians in particular with a way of telling the world that they had come to town, reached the big time, gone pop. These Rhinestone Cowboys have come in for a lot of criticism from those who naively thought that country music could somehow remain pure within the razzle dazzle of the pop world.

Like SEQUINS, rhinestones radiate light patterns which work well under spotlights and make performers appear larger than life.

Opposite page
Top left: Slim Whitman – definitive rhinestone cowboy, 1981
Top right: Porter Wagoner with studs as well as rhinestones, 1979
Bottom right: Elvis Presley in the outlandish outfit he wore for one of his final concert tours
Bottom left: Diana Ross sparkling in 1971
This page
Liberace, one of the most OTT dressers in popular entertainment (even the shoes have rhinestones!)

RIPPED AND TORN

Richard Hell (ex-Neon Boys, Television and Heartbreakers) is frequently credited with the invention of the ripped t-shirt but verifying this claim is almost as difficult as finding out who invented the wheel. What we can be sure of, however, is that 'Rip it up' is one of rock's great war cries. Punks, post-punks and proto-punks such as Hell, Alice Cooper (see LEATHER) and Marc Bolan simply decided to take things literally. With Theresa Coburn's designs for Specimen one wonders if things can go any further.

Right: Marc Bolan of T. Rex during his punk phase in the mid 1970s
Far right: Adam during The Ants' early days in tastefully ripped t-shirt from Malcolm McLaren and Vivienne Westwood's Sex boutique, 1977
Bottom right: Johnny Melton of Specimen in ripped rubber, 1983
Bottom: 'Jaggy-Dress' in 1983 SOUNDS ad
Below: Wendy O. Williams, 1980

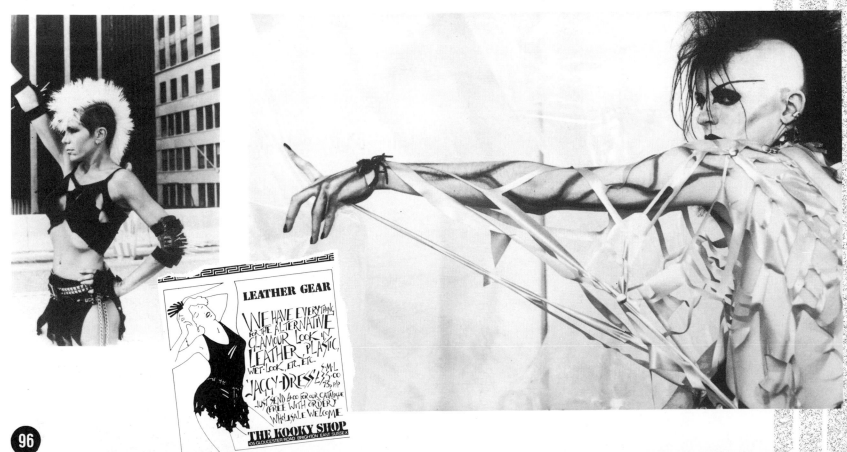

RUFFLES

Although contemporary pop stars such as David Bowie and Boy George have bent over backwards to effect via their dress styles a redefinition of masculinity, we should also pause to reflect on the fact that, in a less provocative manner, pop music has always been in the business of challenging our society's definition of male and female behaviour. The ruffled dress shirt, worn with evening jacket and bow tie, was one of the first great pop styles and yet even today males who are not engaged in show business may feel hesitant about putting on such a 'feminine' garment. For musicians in the cabaret and club side of the business, the rule seems to be 'when in doubt put ruffles on it – then add sequins, rhinestones and embroidery to taste'.

Left: The Shangri-Las with matching outfits and poses, 1965
Centre left: Donna Summer on 'I Remember Yesterday', 1977
Top left: Country star Dottie West
Top right: Sweaty but unbowed, the irrepressible Meatloaf, 1981
Centre right: 1969 NME ad for Carnaby Cavern – suppliers to everyone from The Kinks to Status Quo
Above: Junex ad NME, 1965
Right: 'The Killer' Jerry Lee Lewis in formal attire on 'My Fingers Do The Talkin', 1983

SCARVES

Normally worn for warmth, the scarf would seem to offer little to the pop performer sweating under stage lighting, and yet they appear all over the pop world. Aside from their decorative purpose, these bits of cloth have often been employed as mops for sweaty brows (cf. Meatloaf), tokens to throw to a few ecstatic fans (cf. Presley's final concert tour of America), headbands, hats and even as temporary masks. There's a lot of things you can do with a scarf and pop people have tried most of them. Fans have also frequently got into the act by waving appropriately decorated scarves at their heroes in the manner of football fans. Usually this is simply a scarf with the pop star's name on it but when, for example, Rod Stewart gives a concert in Scotland the entire audience seems to be sinking in a sea of waving tartan scarves.

Clockwise from top right:
Rod Stewart in classic 1970s pose with tartan scarf as a symbol of his Scottish roots
Chris Cross of Ultravox with scarf as neckerchief
War with scarves as outlaw masks
The Five Keys in the late 1940s and early 1950s wore their scarves as cravats.
'Miami' Steve Van Zandt of Little Steven and the Disciples of Soul on 'Men Without Women' wears his scarf as headgear

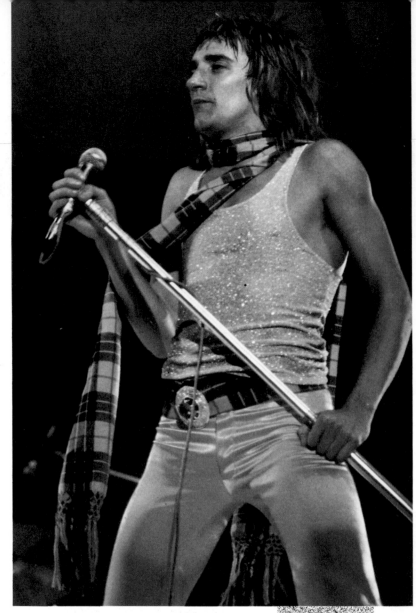

Similar in effect to rhinestones – though they can be knitted or sewn on to fabric to make a solid scaley mass – sequins are another great showbiz device. These small, usually circular, pieces of metal or plastic make a glinting metallic priestess of Tina Turner or a platinum king of Rick James. All that glistens is not gold but it looks great and sometimes sells a lot of records.

**Clockwise from top left:
Tina Turner; The Three Degrees;
The Sequence; Sylvester**

Below: Esther Phillips who began her career in the early 1950s as Little Esther with the Johnny Otis Show
Top right: French pop star Sylvie Vartan, 1979
Bottom right: Jean Carn on 'Trust Me', 1982
Bottom centre: Bonnie Pointer who started with The Pointer Sisters backing artists such as Esther Phillips and went solo in the late 1970s, pictured here in 1980

I DONT WANT THE NIGHT TO END
Sylvie Vartan

In the early days of the cinema, film stars often had to perform under such harsh lighting that their eyes became strained. This led to their wearing sunglasses in situations where they would not normally be required. It was presumed by the public that it was a debauched lifestyle which produced eyestrain, or that some of Hollywood's stars were vampire-like creatures of the night. Eventually sunglasses came to signify simply that one *was* a star, an assumption which was exploited by would-be stars. Then came pop stars and pop styles to edge film stars and film styles out of the limelight, but sunglasses and their implications of stardom remained to provide a link between these two types of entertainment. Since then musicians have taken things one step further, widening the horizons of style possibilities. Some shades have become shorthand for certain pop personalities. There follows on the next two pages, therefore, a quick test of who wears what style. . . .

**Clockwise from left:
Little Stevie Wonder in classic 1963 shot
Graham Parker, 1982
'X-Spex the original wraparounds!' from Kanda Fashions ad in NME, 1982
Radiospecs ad from NME, 1968 – the forerunner of the Walkman
Tata Vega in distinctive heart shaped shades, 1979**

X-SPEX
THE ORIGINAL WRAPAROUNDS!

SHINY BLACK
SUNGLASSES
ONLY £2

AVAILABLE NOW!

TRANSISTOR RADIO
& SUNGLASSES
COMBINED
* HI-FI TONE
* INC. BATTERY
* 12 MONTH GUARANTEE
AMAZING VALUE
95'.
inc. Postage

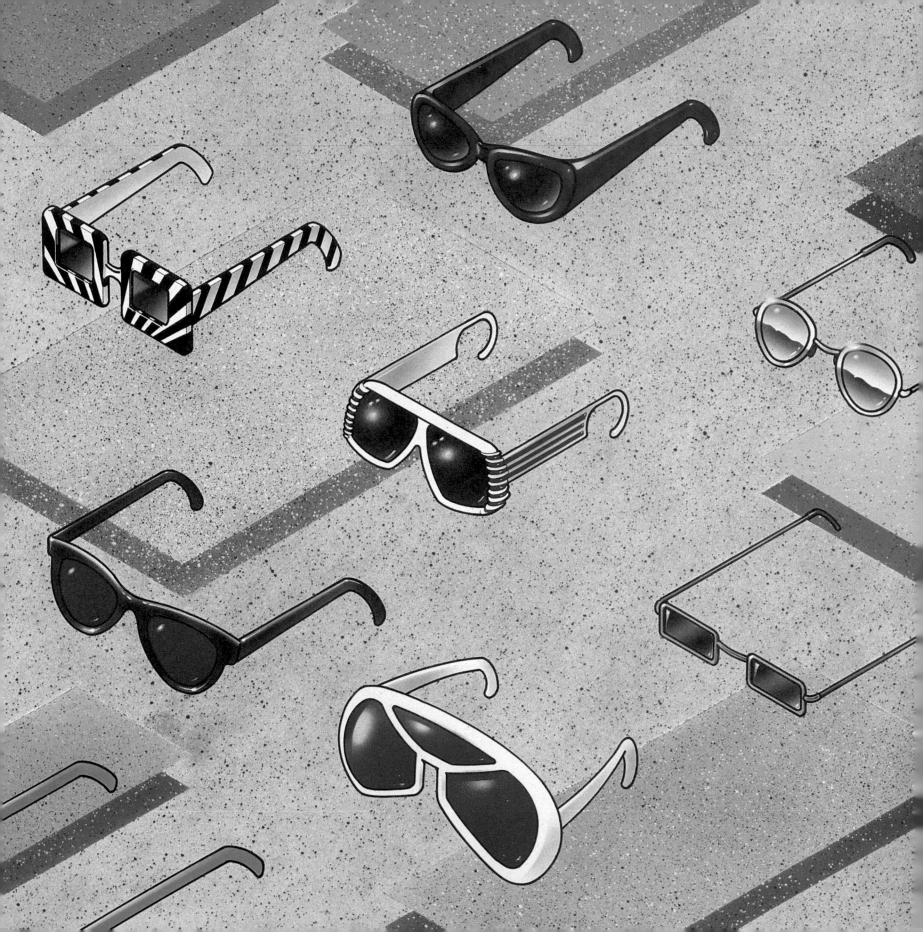

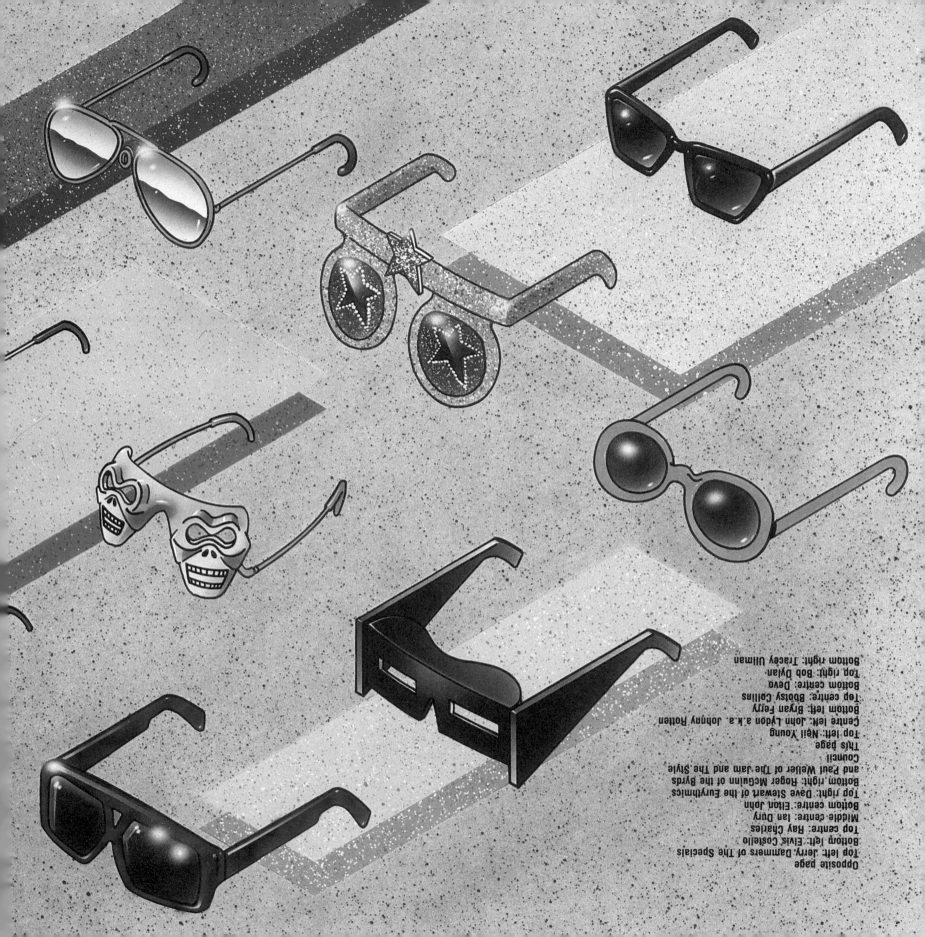

The mark of the outsider, the religious extremist, the insane, the diseased and the convict – and a lot of bother to maintain – the shaved head isn't for everyone, although a surprising number of early eighties pop personalities have chosen to adopt it. In the seventies, Isaac Hayes and a few other soul artists went in for this ultimate reaction to the hippy look. Long before, however, blues singer Eddie 'Cleanhead' Vinson had pioneered the look – even singing about how his hair had been worn away by the constant petting by his lady friends. He made a feature of what was probably a natural 'affliction', one which a later generation would recreate with a razor.

Clockwise from top left:
Genesis P-Orridge and Peter Christopherson of Psychic TV on 'Force The Hand Of Chance'
Wattie of Exploited
Sal Solo of Classix Nouveaux
Riff Regan of London
Isaac Hayes on 'Hot Buttered Soul', 1969
Fatty Buster Bloodvessel of Bad Manners

Pop people wear short shorts, long shorts, baggy shorts, track shorts, Bermuda shorts, tight shorts (sometimes known as hot pants), cut-off shorts, etc. Some people look silly in them. On some they look sexy. Somebody even wrote a song about them. For a pop style there can be no greater accolade.

Left: Diana Ross on 'Diana Ross' in cut off jeans, 1970
Top left: The Sensational Alex Harvey Band showing a lot of leg in the mid 1970s
Top right: Sting of the Police, 1982
Above: Captain Sensible happy talking in Bermudas, 1982

105

Near left: Lulu in original 1960s hot pants
Above: Claudia Barry in 1970s disco style
Far left: Tracey Ullman in an 1980s parody of 1970s glam

SKIN

In the annals of pop styles, what doesn't get worn often causes even more fuss than what does. Flashing flesh has long been a stock in trade of the pop business, especially since the day Jim 'I wanted to see what it would look like in the spotlight' Morrison unzipped his jeans. A bit of leg and cleavage advanced the careers of many pre-rock female singers but rock's contribution has been to let the boys in on the act while the girls go all the way. Today the practice of pop stars revealing themselves on stage has spread far and wide, from Tom Jones ritually unbuttoning his ruffled shirt to the waist to Adam Ant performing stripteases for his audiences to Annabella Lwin baring all for the sake of a good picture and a lot of publicity.

Above: Kate Garner of Haysi Fantayzee
Top: Bowie as a Diamond Dog, 1974
Right: Bow Wow Wow cover art for 'See Jungle'. Annabella commented "It's not really pornographic . . . A lot of people reckon it's a hell of a lot better than the painting."
Far right: Wendy O. Williams of the Plasmatics with Lemmy of Motorhead, 1982

Some pop people are literally out of this world – or at least they would like us to think they are. Derived from the flying suit, heavy with science fiction connotations, space suits have cropped up throughout the last few decades – one of the first space suited groups, the 1962 Spotniks, wore full suits and clear helmets like those seen in the early science fiction films – but so far they haven't been much taken up as street styles by the fans.

Above: Smiling spacemen Sho-Nuff
Top left: French group Les Rockets complete with metal painted pates, 1976
Top right: Landscape's original line up, 1980
Right: Klaus Meime of the Scorpions with phallic ray gun, 1982

SPORTSWEAR

Traditionally the term 'sportswear' refers to any casual dress evolved from athletic origins. As fashion historians have noted, an astounding proportion of clothes owe something to sporting roots. 'The history of any male garment is inevitably the same. It begins being a sports suit; it is designed to provide ease of operation in some comparatively active pursuit. It ends by being 'dress clothes'.'* The same can be said of modern dress for women, which owes much to garments originally designed for bicycling, tennis, hunting, skiing etc. Thus in this sense of the term, most of the things we wear and most of the clothing in this book could be called sportswear.

That said, it is important to note how pop styles in the eighties reflect our society's recent swing towards a preoccupation – approaching a religion – with sport and physical fitness. Sportswear in this context refers not to clothes which have evolved from such origins but to garments in which one actually performs athletic endeavours.

Just about the only thing that hippies, mods, teds, headbangers and punks have in common is a disdain for all things relating to exercise. Yet the gymnasium, the dance class, the swimming pool and aerobics classes have now influenced the pop stage and videos. The ideology which produced 'Muscles' and 'Physical' as hit records is a far cry from Bob Dylan in shades in a smoky Greenwich Village club, Johnny Rotten's decaying grin or even Frank Sinatra having a smoke and a quick drink between songs.

*Dress, James Laver, John Murray, London, 1966

Above: Neville Staples of Fun Boy Three in track suit bottom and sports socks
Right: Olivia Newton-John gets physical in a sweat band
Bottom right: Beggar & Co. on 'We All Work Out'
Below: Slik in baseball gear in the mid 1970s when second hand American sports clothes were the rage in Britain
Bottom left: Junior with pedal power

Far left: Dreams in th
boxing ring
Left: Carlene Carter a
a cheerleader

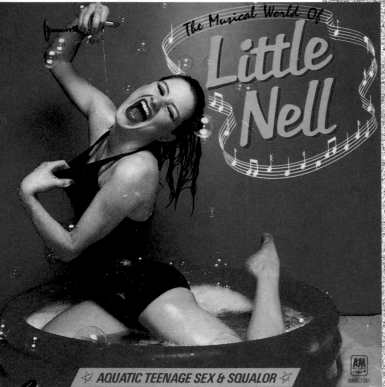

Far left: Little Nell
does the swim in the
mid 1970s
Left: The Ritchie
Family, all-round
sports in 1979
Above: Girl in baseb
gear for 'Thru the
Twilite' picture
disc, 1981

Studs are literally heavy metal.

According to Pod of Easyrider Leather Goods (47b Virginia Street, Southport, Lancs.) 'The studded belt originally had domed studs and was developed by GI dispatch riders in World War II to protect the hip and lower back bones if a rider skidded. The belts looked good and very butch and became popular with bikers in the US after the war – particularly the Hells Angels. When heavy rock bands came along the bikers took to them in such a committed way that their culture affected the bands' stage presentation, dress and gross!! behaviour. With the bands wearing biker clothing, studs became and remain a fashion with fans. Much of punk dress and behaviour is derived from the biker cult. Butterfly pointed studs are particularly in fashion with them but belts made with these are no good as protective clothing. Studded belts are an example of the street influencing the dress of the bands who created a fashion.'

Above: Punk bondage and studs from 1983 Left and right: Lita Ford (ex-Runaways) and friends in heavy rock studs from 'Out for Blood', 1983

Above: Motorhead
fighting off
the fans
Left: Rob Halford
of Judas Priest
Below left: Black
leather studded
belt and wristband
from 1up Trading
Co. SOUNDS, 1980
Bottom left: 'Real
machismo punk style'
wristband from Seagull
Trading Company
NME, 1978
Right: Lou Reed
on 'Live'

Black Leather Studded
Belt £3.00
Leather Dog Collar
(studded) £3.00
Wristbands £1.00!

45 C

112

The suit never needed pop music to ensure its popularity but pop has in its history shone a spotlight on certain specific types of suits and in some cases made them famous. *Zoot suits* came into being hand in hand with jazz-based pop music. They were distinctive because of their outrageously baggy, high-waisted trousers and finger-tip-length jackets and were worn with a key chain, pocket watch and a lot of flair. Their popularity faded in the fifties but was revived and revered recently by musicians such as Chris Sullivan of Blue Rondo A La Turk.

The *mod suits* of the sixties were lean and tight, pretty much perfect opposites of the zoot. Based on sharp Italian styling, they were brought into fashion by the original British mods and by American modern jazz musicians. This suit dominated the sixties until collars and trimmings began to grow and get fussy, which destroyed the clean, trim spirit of the design. One variation on the mod suit was the *collarless suit* which became known as the 'Beatle suit' (see INTRODUCTION). Although short lived, its space-age lines represented one kind of perfection. Another important variant of the mod suit was made of a woven material called *Tonic* which appeared one colour when looked at from one direction and another colour when viewed from a different angle. This *two-tone* quality would later be linked with a whole school of music which also took the term to denote a black and white racial mix in the bands' members and musical roots.

Top right: Louis Jordan's 1940s zoot
Top left: Sullivan's Suits NME, 1982
Centre: George Melly, early 1980s
Above: Brian Poole and The Tremeloes, mid 1960s
Right: Carnaby Cavern ad SOUNDS, 1981
Left: Bob Crosby, 1930-40s band leader
Far left: Slades of Piccadilly NME, 1955

SOUL-SKA!

ORIGINAL ROCKSTEADY
Byron Lee's Allstars
+Friends.

VISTA SOUNDS

The Glitter Band

HEY!

Above left: The classic ska suit
Above right: The 1970s glam suit
Left: Kid Creole's safari suit, 1982
Right: Bowie's 1974 suit
Below: The style was so strong that
even into the 1980s readers of NME
wanted to look like the Thin White
Duke courtesy of Christopher Robin
Opposite: Showaddywaddy's
subtle drapes

DAVID
LIVE

S LOWEST PRIC

BOWIE

Bowie Jacket (as David Live LP)
Black, white, navy, grey, brown,
yellow, red and lt blue. 32" to 42"
chest. **Only £28.50**
8 pleat Trousers colours as
Jackets. 24" to 38" waist. **Just
£14.95**
20 pleat Trousers. Colours as
Jackets. 24" to 38" waist. **Only
£16.95**
**As Suit with 8 pleat Trouser
£42.50**
With 20 pleat £43.50
NEW
Bowie Satin Jacket black, white,
red, navy and grey. 32" to 42"
chest. **£34.50**
8 pleat Trouser colours as Jacket
24" to 38" waist. **£17.95**
20 pleat Satin Trouser colours as
Jackets. 24" to 38" waist. **£19.95**
As Suit with 8 pleat £49.95
With 20 pleats £50.95
Short collar shirts in white only.
14½" to 16½". **£5.00**
Satin Bowie Ties Colours as Suit
£3.50

Right: The Jam, 1977
Below right: Carnaby Cavern ad from NME, 1971
Top left: Rod 'The Mod' Stewart in 1964
Centre left: 'Cool colours, wash and wear fabric and Harry Fenton styling gives any man the sharp look' in 'white, lemon and pale blue' NME, 1967
Bottom row from left:
'Tonic suits' by Retro from NME, 1979
Madness logo on 'One Step Beyond', 1979
An earlier Harry Fenton ad from DISC, 1964
The Escorts, 1964 picture from Edsel's 'From The Blue Angel'

THE TOP GROUPS ARE DRESSED BY HARRY FENTON

SHAFTESBURY AVE. CORNER OF WARDOUR ST. BRANCHES EVERYWHERE

SWEATERS

These days the handmade sweater is the treasure of the rich, the lucky or the skilled. It is most closely identified with safe folksy singers such as Val Doonican and Perry Como, and with those 'hand made by my Granny' associations, sweaters usually convey a warm, cosy, cuddly image. Exceptions to this rule are turtle-necks, which became associated with beatnik dives back in the days when only the avant garde didn't wear ties, and early punk mohair jumpers which had such a loose knit that a high degree of nipple visibility was inevitable.

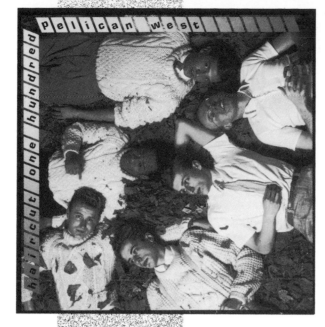

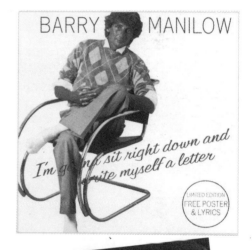

Clockwise from top left:
Haircut 100 in chunky cable-knit Arran sweaters, 1982
The Commodores in tight fitting turtle-necks, early 1970s
Barry Manilow in smart pastel patterned sweater, 1982
The Beverley Sisters, who pioneered casual dress for pop stars, on their 1950s TV series, shown here in musical note motif numbers
The Shadows looking casual in woolly sweaters in 1962 for their first album without Cliff Richard

TARTAN

Often referred to in the US as tartan plaid or just plaid, tartan derives from Scottish clans who use different designs to denote different families. It has been surprisingly popular even among non-Scottish pop people, such as the Northern Soul boys from Wigan, whilst some Scottish musicians have nearly used the stuff to death in an attempt to deify their roots, e.g., The Bay City Rollers and Rod Stewart (see SCARVES). Some punks in the late seventies showed the delightful kitch effect which can be achieved by following such an obsession to its logical conclusion.

Bottom left: Tartan was popular with early rock and rollers and revived by The Dynamite Band in 1982
Top: The Bay City Rollers took tartan to an extreme none but their fans cared to follow
Below: John Lydon of Public Image Ltd, in post-punk tartan
Bottom: Similar tartan suits were available from Carnaby Cavern in 1980 through ads in SOUNDS

THE DYNAMITE BAND

Rockin' is our Business

TATTOOS

Not very long ago if a musician had a tattoo it was a carefully guarded secret. Janis Joplin was one of the first big stars to go public when she appeared on a chat show saying that she had just acquired two new tattoos; a tattooed bracelet around her wrist and another in a private place, just for friends and lovers to appreciate. This was shocking stuff. Tattoos have traditionally had a bad reputation and those who wanted to preserve their good name kept their mouths shut about their body art. But now pop stars such as the Stray Cats even credit their tattoo artist Denis Cockell on their record sleeves, and Rose Tattoo have an ex-professional tattooist actually in the group. Fans increasingly have names of favourite musicians tattooed on their persons – probably not such a good idea given the fact that pop allegiances are often so fickle. But we should, I think, tip our hats to those old-time rockers who sport first-rate portraits of their lifetime heroes. Let us hope that they see fit to stipulate in their wills that their skins be given to national art galleries – if only for the fun of seeing what the galleries' directors would decide to do with such modern masterpieces.

On the following page we have another game! Can you identify which of the tattoos illustrated here appear or appeared on which pop stars' bodies? Answers upside down at the bottom of the page.

Top: Rose Tattoo are 'Scarred for life', 1982
Near right: Tattoo transfer ad. NME 1967
Far right: Steve Jones of the Sex Pistols being tattooed by Denis Cockell

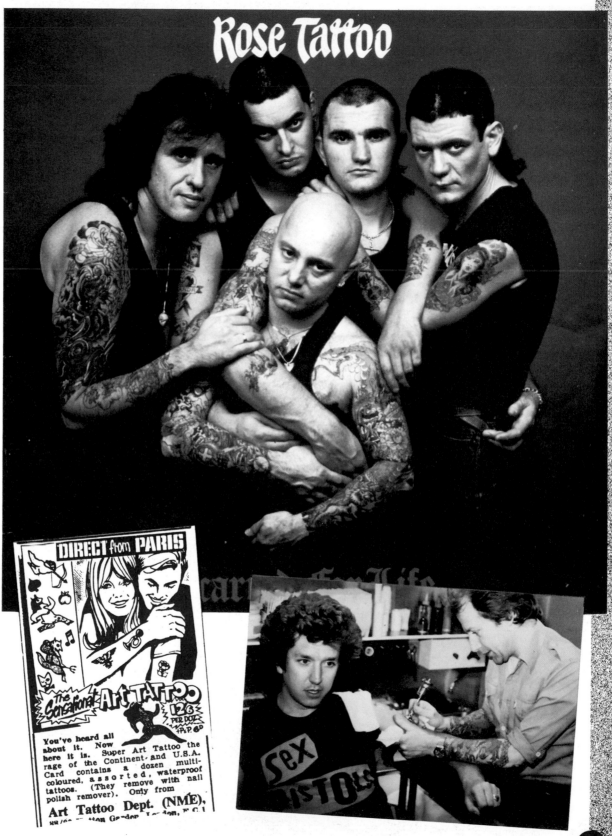

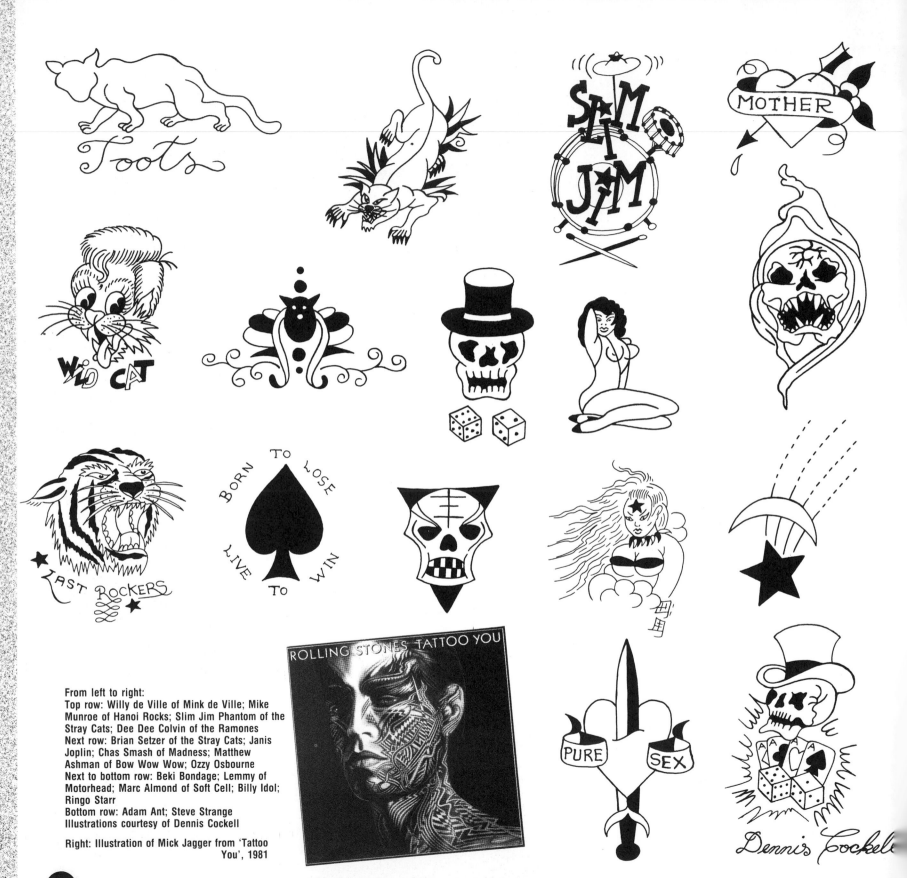

Foots

MOTHER

WILD CAT

SLIM JIM

BORN TO LOSE LIVE TO WIN

LAST ROCKERS

PURE SEX

ROLLING STONES TATTOO YOU

From left to right:
Top row: Willy de Ville of Mink de Ville; Mike Munroe of Hanoi Rocks; Slim Jim Phantom of the Stray Cats; Dee Dee Colvin of the Ramones
Next row: Brian Setzer of the Stray Cats; Janis Joplin; Chas Smash of Madness; Matthew Ashman of Bow Wow Wow; Ozzy Osbourne
Next to bottom row: Beki Bondage; Lemmy of Motorhead; Marc Almond of Soft Cell; Billy Idol; Ringo Starr
Bottom row: Adam Ant; Steve Strange
Illustrations courtesy of Dennis Cockell

Right: Illustration of Mick Jagger from 'Tattoo You', 1981

Dennis Cockell

Backcombing has often been a female contemporary of the male quiff, with hair spray being used instead of grease. It is true that males such as Little Richard have dabbled in this art, but the supreme practitioners have been women. Especially in the beehive where the hair is sprayed, backcombed and manipulated with care until it reached straight up to the stars, truly wondrous effects have been achieved. Even the less majestic bouffant has aided many pop people by making them seem bigger than they are.

It is interesting how many of pop styles' tricks of the trade – sequins, rhinestones, platform boots, afros, feathers, quiffs, ruffles, studs, zoot suits, hats, fur coats, bold tartan checks, lumberjack shirts, etc. – have, like hair

Clockwise from top:
The Ronettes, 1964
Kate Pierson (left) and Cindy Wilson of the B-52's from 'Wild Planet', 1980
Ike Turner from 'Ike Turner's Kings of Rythm Vol. 1', early 1950s
The Velvelettes, early 1960s
Mary Wells from 'Mary Wells' Greatest Hits', early 1960s

teasing, the effect of making the star or would-be star appear larger than life.

Mari Wilson herself has kindly supplied us with some helpful hints on how you can emulate her beehive.

'Essentials for a good beehive:
1 a daily supply of extra-hold hair spray
2 electric rollers
3 plenty of backcombing
4 at least fifty hair pins
5 a flower in the pleat at the back

Directions: Put rollers in. When you have taken them out, backcomb to buggery. Spray all over with hair spray, mould and grip.'

In contrast, punk and post-punk musicians and fans have shown how new effects can be achieved using this old trick.

This page:
Clockwise from above:
Terry Hall of Fun Boy Three
Debbie Harry of Blondie in teased wig
Limahl (ex-Kajagoogoo)
Illustration from The Gonads' 'Pure Punk for Row People'
Opposite page:
Mari Wilson before she moved on from her famous beehive

Patti Smith · Horses

A sign of conformity and respectability, ties are antithetical to the spirit of rock and roll – unless they are extreme or unusual. Happily there are many such styles to choose from. The *kipper* is, like its namesake, extremely wide and is often in garish colours or decorated with hand-painted designs. First worn with zoot suits, they acquired their name (probably only in Britain, home of the kipper) in the sixties when they were revived in Swinging London. *Slim Jims* represent the opposite extreme – thin, neat and very mod/modern jazz/Ivy League. The *bootlace* is made of a cord or leather thong which is threaded through an ornamental clasp usually made of metal. These ties were worn by cowboys who often had their brand decorating the clasp. Singing cowboys brought the style to pop music where first country musicians and later rockabillies took to them in a big way. Finally there is the *bow tie* which was a mainstay of pre-rock pop but which is increasingly appreciated by rock musicians for its flair and distinctiveness – especially when left nonchalantly untied.

Clockwise from above left:
Joe Jackson's Jumpin' Jive in brightly-patterned 1940s style wide ties
Patti Smith on 'Horses' with thin tie
The Manish Boys in paisley and floral ties in 1965 with Davy Jones before he became David Bowie
Judy of the Bellestars in string tie
Joe Ely in string tie on the cover of 'Musta Notta Gotta Lotta'

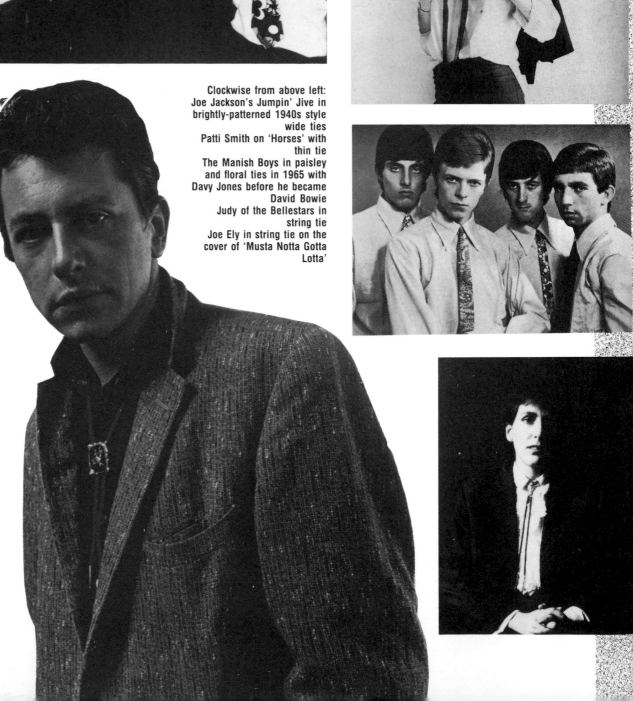

Clockwise from top left:
The Stargazers in tuxedos and bow ties
Jools Holland, musician and TV presenter, sporting Western style tie
Paul McCartney figuring out how to fix his bow tie
Klaus Nomi in futuristic formal attire
Brian Downey of Thin Lizzy wearing lurex Western tie
Melba Moore in formals and bow tie

TIGHT TROUSERS

When pop musicians have not been concerned with extremely baggy trousers they have been obsessed with extremely tight ones. When I bought my first pair of *drainpipes* as a teenager my father objected that they 'Show everything you've got' which was, of course, the point. P. J. Proby was better known for splitting his than for his singing talents. *Pedal pushers* for girls, were shorter and made of thinner material which could show even more. Glam saw the boys fighting back by co-opting for themselves thin, revealing fabrics such as satin. With technological advances in stretch fabrics happening in time for punk, people such as Nina Hagen could look almost as if they had no trousers on at all, while in the disco era, spandex left almost as little to the imagination. Today it is the heavy metallurgists who keep the tradition of tight trousers alive.

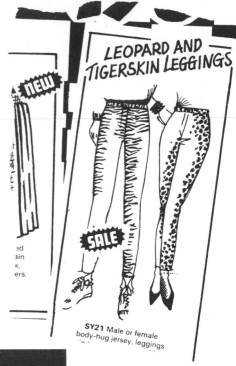

LEOPARD AND TIGERSKIN LEGGINGS

SY21 Male or female body-hug jersey, leggings

PRINTOUT PROMOTIONS

Clockwise from top left:
Gary Moore in stretch black plastic drainpipes
Post-punk leggings from Gringos NME, 1980
Printout Promotions ad from SOUNDS, 1982
Peter 'Biff' Byford of Saxon reveals one reason why tight trousers are so popular
P. J. Proby with tight cords still in one piece, mid 1960s

Opposite page:
Bottom: Little Eva, who broke into the music business by baby-sitting for Carole King, who with her husband Gerry Goffin wrote 'The Locomotion', Little Eva's 1962 big hit. Shown here in fine cord pedal pushers

Top row from left:
The Coconuts in pedal pushers on Kid Creole's 'Tropical Gangsters'
Nina Hagen in punk plastic
Bonnie Tyler in pedal pushers
Drainpipe jeans from Husklynn Ltd. SOUNDS, 1980
Right: Kate Robbins in shiny spandex
Far right: Dogtooth check ski pants and striped pedal pushers from Individual Trading Company SOUNDS, 1980

TRANSEX

No one could say that pop music alone had brought about the changes in attitude to male and female behaviour which our society has been caught up in for the last couple of decades. But neither can we ignore the part pop people have played. David Bowie's significance in this has been discussed in the MAKE-UP section. Although he is the best known of the pop world's gender benders a lot happened before he even bought his first eyeliner. *Any* male performer who dressed up and simply let it be known that he cared about his appearance was not, and for some will never be, 'a real man'. Even someone as butch as Elvis Presley

was, when wearing rhinestones or too tight jeans, suspect.

In Britain the Beverley Sisters (see GROUP UNIFORM) were the first women singers to appear on television in trousers, which caused a lot of fuss. Today you might think anything goes, but you would be wrong. In America, Boy George of Culture Club and Ann Lennox of the Eurythmics have had their TV appearances restricted by cable TV executives who thought they were transvestites. Aside from the fact that they are excellent vocalists, both are making important non-verbal statements about the unnecessarily restricted nature of gender roles.

Above: David Bowie looking stunning in a sequined dress for the 'Boys Keep Swingin' video, 1979
Right: Grace Jones 'Nightclubbing', 1981
Far right: Jayne County, previously Wayne County, on 'Rock 'n' Roll Resurrection', 1980
Top right: Marilyn looking remarkably like his namesake at the Blitz club in 1979 when it was the hang-out for Steve Strange, Boy George, Spandau Ballet and many other stars of the 1980s

Previous page:
'Some Girls' including The Rolling Stones, 1978
This page:
Below: Ann Lennox of The Eurythmics – a performer who adroitly experiments and plays with female gender roles
Right: Another expert in gender confusion, Ronny in dress and suit from Anthony Price

Above: The New York Dolls all tarted up for their first album in 1973
Below: Boy George confusing the public at London's Hampstead Heath fair back in the days before he was a star, 1980
Below left: Keith Moon of The Who and Eric Clapton make a charming couple, 1971

TUXEDOS

Some post-punks adopted the tuxedo out of context as a kind of subversive joke and a few new romantic crooners took it to heart, but its continuing survival has been mainly dependent upon the ongoing non-rock pop scene.

Clockwise from top left:
The Four Tops, 1965
Bryan Ferry on 'Another Time, Another Place', 1974
John King of Gang of Four, 1980
Hi-Style Overalls ad for musicians' work-wear NME, 1970
The Motams, 1982

Now and throughout most of pop history, the shiny rounded lapels of the tuxedo have been the sign of a classy act. Rock and roll initially rejected this tradition by defining itself as rough, tough and common, but significant exceptions soon developed, especially among the black artists of the Motown and do-wop eras who rediscovered the tux and class. The hard rock of the late sixties spurned it once more and glam rock in the seventies sought to create a bolder kind of glamour.

The long history of military and civil uniform design and the way it often serves as a reservoir of male flamboyance make uniforms good source material for street and pop style. The sixties in particular saw this rich and inexpensive (in second-hand shops and army surplus shops) resource exploited. At first the spirit of this military fancy dress party was one of light parody and fun, but when opposition to the war in Vietnam became part of rock's political posture, the wearing of military styles came to signify a serious put-down of all things military. Since Vietnam, the edge of anti-war protest has grown less sharp (anti-bomb protests are a more immediate eighties concern) and camouflage prints, gold piping and such like are now worn more for aesthetic than political reasons.

Paramount Presents
ELVIS PRESLEY
IN
G.I. BLUES
A HAL WALLIS PRODUCTION
Co-starring
JULIET PROWSE
TECHNICOLOR*
Directed By
Norman Taurog

SIDE I **Tonight Is So Right for Love** (Wayne, Silver)
What's She Really Like (Wayne, Silver)
Frankfort Special (Wayne, Edwards)
Wooden Heart (Wise, Weisman, Twomey, Kaempfert)

SIDE II

"Stereo records give full stereo reproduction when played on a stereo record player. They can be played on most modern mono record players fitted with a light-weight tone arm and pick-up head and the sound reproduction will be monaural. If you have doubts and wish to avoid damaging your equipment or records, consult your dealer."

...ISION, RCA HOUSE, CURZON STREET, LONDON W.1.

Garrodprint Ltd

THE **MONKEES**
I'M A BELIEVER EP

£9·95   Mike Corbett
CAVALRY STYLE
SHIRT
100% COTTON SHIRT features
Short Collar, Bib Front,
Stud Fastening. Colours—
BLACK, WHITE, GREY or
AIRFORCE BLUE.
Sizes— S. M. L.
Please state size & second colour choice
and allow 14 days for delivery.
Send cheques or PO's for £9·95 to
MIKE CORBETT   17 Belvedere,
Lansdown Rd. Bath, Avon.

Achtung
2 × 2½p STAMPS gets you my
ILLUSTRATED LISTS OF T-SHIRTS,
POSTERS, MEDALS, BADGES,
& SEW-ON PATCHES.

105. 55p SWASTIKA NICKEL·RIBBON
107. 55p IRON CROSS NICKEL/BLACK WITH RIBBON
121. 'ZODIAC' STAR £1·00 NICKEL/BLACK + CHAIN
113. £1·00 ANGELS CROSS NICKEL/BLACK WITH RIBBON
114. 85p 'EAGLE RING' NICKEL/BLACK
102. 85p 'BREAST EAGLE' NICKEL PLATED
111. £1·00 'LUFTWAFFE' CLOTH EAGLE EMBROIDERED SILVER ON BLUE
103. £1·00 4" 'CAP EAGLE' NICKEL PLATED
109. £1·00 NAVAL CLOTH EAGLE EMBROIDERED GOLD ON BLACK
161. £1·00 U.S.A. ARMY CLOTH SEW-ON PATCHES. FOUR COLOURFULL SHOULDER BADGES. ALL DIFFERENT. £1·00 THE LOT!!

PAUL KINCH MAIL ORDER 4 CARDIFF RD LUTON. BEDS.

NEW MUSIC CENTRE

Top: Elvis Presley models various military uniforms from his 1961 movie 'G.I. Blues'
Above: Mike Corbett ad from NME, 1981
Left: The Monkees in cavalry/confederate shirts, 1967
Right: Nazi badges and insignia from Paul Kinch ad in NME, 1973

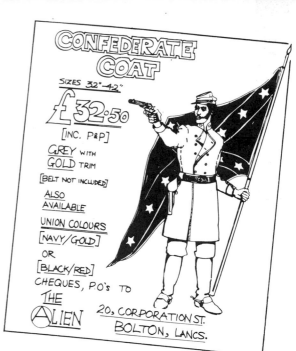

Left: Elton John with medals, braid and epaulettes during
his 1982 tour
Above: I Was Lord Kitchener's Valet ad from NME, 1967
Right: The Alien ad from NME, 1981
Below: The Beatles in their 'Sergeant Pepper's Lonely
Hearts Club Band' uniforms of brightly coloured satin,
John with flowers, Ringo with sequined tie, 1967

Top row from left:
Peter Grant ad from NME, 1967
Eddie Tudorpole of Tenpole Tudor
brings a new meaning to the phrase
'heavy metal'
Steve Strange of Visage dressed to
kill in leather uniform with
epaulettes
Below: Duran Duran ready to do battle
in the charts

Above: Snuky Tate in high
necked military tunic on
'Babylon Under Pressure',
1982
Left: A similar jacket was
available to readers of NME
from Silverman's back in 1967

VESTS

CLIFF RICHARD ★ THE SHADOWS
SUMMER HOLIDAY

CLIFF RICHARD and THE SHADOWS

SUMMER HOLIDAY

The popularity in the rock world of the vest (or as it is known in America, the undershirt) offers another example of underwear becoming respectable as outer garments (see LINGERIE). Respectability did not come instantly and for a time this flaunting of 'private' garments in public places was a useful tool of rock and roll rebellion. Today, t-shirts have become so ubiquitous and socially acceptable that there is nothing shocking about wearing them or any other type of vest – except perhaps for the racy *string vest* which was so boldly introduced by Cliff Richard in 1963 and which still carries enough symbolic punch to be adopted by punk bands. The *grandad vest* is now long forgotten while the fitness boom has recently popularised tight, stretchy athletic or *muscle vests* (see SPORTSWEAR).

Clockwise from above:
Cliff Richard keeps cool in a string vest in his 1963 film 'Summer Holiday'
Lynval Golding of Fun Boy Three in a 1980s version of the string vest
Glynn Barber of Chron Gen in a punk style black string vest, 1981
Diana Ross in a button front grandad vest, 1980
'Be a smash at every freak-out!' in a 'fabulous button front vest' from GR & DC Enterprises NME, 1969

WAISTCOATS

Also known as vests in America, waistcoats were traditionally worn under a jacket. But in the pop world they have, since the days when Fats Waller pounded a piano in hot dives, been flaunted as outer garments – suggesting gamblers and sharp operators, an attractive image for many pop people. One of the waistcoat's greatest eras was the early seventies when long hair, t-shirts, flares and DENIM waistcoats became the uniform of countless groups and fans.

Clockwise from top left:
Mr. Acker Bilk in fancy brocade waistcoat which, with his customary bowler hat, exemplifies trad jazz
One The Juggler go for a romantic gypsy image in brocade, velvet, and leather waistcoats
Thomas Dolby's eccentric scientist look, complete with tweed waistcoat and watch chain
Leather waistcoat from Branded Discounts Ltd. ad in NME, 1970 – 'Stonehenge Look'?
The Mojos 'Working' in matching suede waistcoats, 1964

Beards, moustaches and sideburns are the most common male pop styles. We have gathered all these separate items together under the heading whiskers because (1) beards, moustaches and sideburns frequently occur in combination and (2) some things, such as the little hairy spot Frank Zappa has cultivated under his lower lip, defy classification. Between them, male ▶

Clockwise from top left:
Thelonious Monk with classic goatee
Billy Gibbons (left) and Dusty Hill of ZZ Top – the third member of the group is, ironically, the much less hirsute Frank Beard
Little Richard with pencil moustache on 'The Georgia Peach'
Jesse Hector of the Gorillas with mutton-chop sideburns
Kenny Rogers with trimmed beard

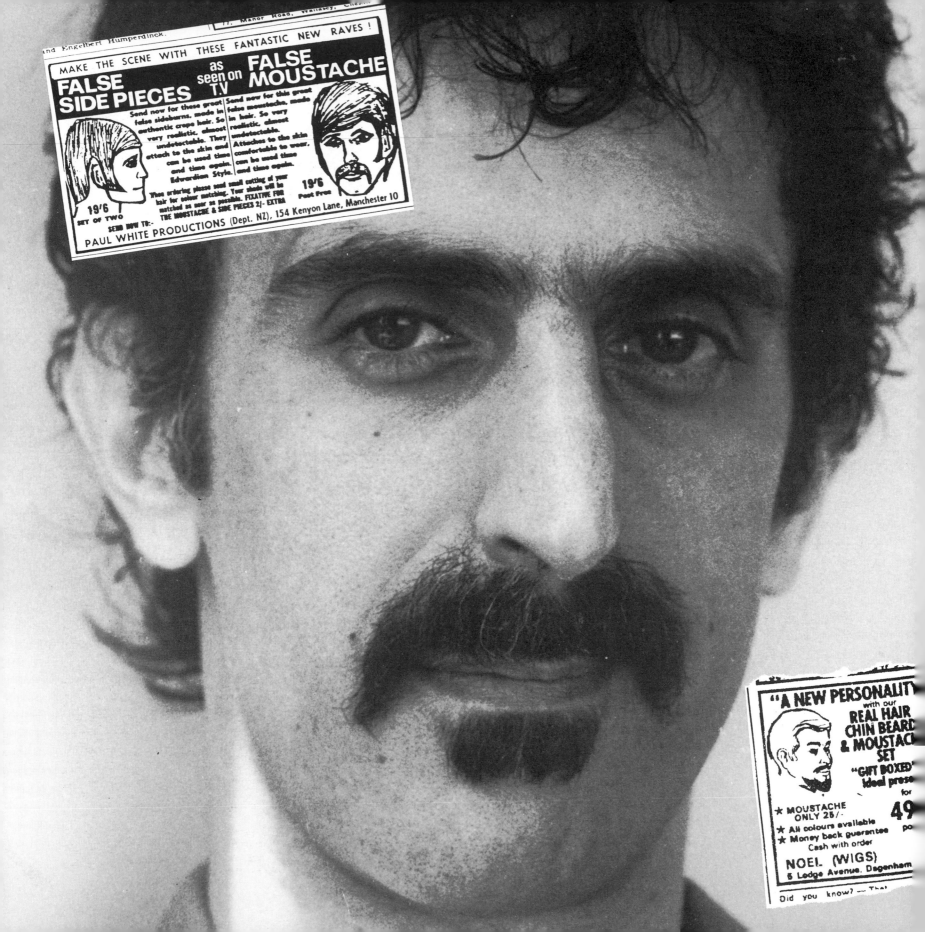

pop musicians have experimented with every conceivable style of whiskers which the human face can produce. Some styles have come to be associated with certain types of music; goatees with folk and jazz, sideburns with rockabilly, full beards with country music and droopy moustaches with psychedelic sounds. By far the biggest new growth area within the category of whiskers is stubble. In the late seventies photos of pop stars in need of a shave suddenly became all the rage. Shades of degeneracy, the resurgence of a macho image and/or the implication that they were just too busy to shave seem to have been the motives for this phenomenon, and now even women such as Ann Lennox (see TRANSEX) seem to be getting in on the act.

Opposite page:
Main picture: Frank Zappa with distinctive moustache and under lip growth
Top: 'Edwardian style false sideburns in authentic crepe hair' and 'almost undetectable false moustache' from Paul White Productions. NME, 1967
Bottom: Fake goatee and moustache set from Noel (Wigs) NME, 1970
This page:
Above: Sam Chatmon challenges ZZ Top in the bushy beard stakes 'Sam Chatmon and His Barbeque Boys'
Top left, top right and centre: Keith Richard, Charlie Watts and Cliff Richard all with bad cases of fashionable 5 o'clock shadow
Centre right: Marvin Gaye with well trimmed beard
Bottom right: Martin Griffin of Hawkwind with impressive handlebar moustache

WIDE COLLARS

Shirt collars were yet another style which started discreetly (see Ricky Nelson) but soon succumbed to the intense visual competition and one-upmanship which is the hallmark of pop styles. Once people had started showing off their shirt collars by wearing them over the top of their jackets there was no stopping the escalation. The primary weapon in this war was size, but musicians such as the Four Tops discovered that by employing contrasting fabrics and patterns for their shirt collars the effect was even greater.

Bottom left: Ricky Nelson on his 'Singles Album'
Top left: 'Star Shirt As supplied to many of Britain's top groups, genuine two-way shirt gives you an adaptable collar from the highest neck fitting yet and unbuttoning down in three stages to a shoulder length Peter Pan collar' Carnaby Cavern ad from NME, 1969
Above: The Joneses
Left: The Four Tops
Below: The Attractions

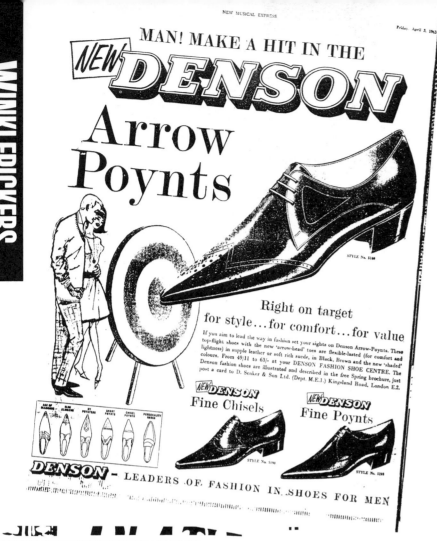

The winkle is a tiny snail-like shellfish which is a favourite snack at English seaside resorts. To pick them out of their shells you need a sharp, pointed object like a pin. Hence the name winklepickers for shoes and boots with extremely pointed toes. Of Italian origin, they first became important as pop styles in the early sixties. By the seventies they were only an amusing anachronism but recently the fashion has revived. The human foot bears little resemblance to the shape of the winklepicker, so a bit of work may be needed to get them on and a high tolerance for discomfort may be needed to keep them there. But, as Joe Jackson says, they sure do look sharp. (By the way, Jackson credits 'Shoes by Denson' on the album sleeve.)

A selection of ads for Denson's Fine Poynts and Fine Chisels
Top left: NME, 1963
Top right: NME, 1964
Bottom left: NME, 1965
Bottom centre: NME, 1978
Centre right: NME, 1978
Bottom right: Cover of Joe Jackson's 'Look Sharp!', 1979

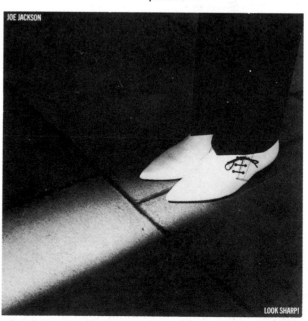

Motorcycle culture and the modern trouser fly brought the zip into the weird world of pop styles. Not much attention was paid to them until Andy Warhol, commissioned to design the 'Sticky Fingers' album sleeve for the Rolling Stones, was acute enough to spotlight the zipped/unzipped crotch (the zip on the original cover actually worked) as a symbol of the Stones' image. A few years later punk musicians and fans celebrated the zip, along with the safety-pin, as a decoration and installed as many as possible wherever possible.

Above: Cover of The Rolling Stones' 'Sticky Fingers', 1971
Bottom far right: Kahn and Bell (now Kahniverous of The Great Gear Market in the Kings Road), ad from SOUNDS, 1980
Top left: Tyneway Trading ad from NME, 1982
Right: Sylvester, 1983
Main picture: Roger Daltrey – from a series of pictures taken to publicise 'One Of The Boys' in 1977, in which he pulls off surprisingly effective personifications of many radically different pop styles. The series could be seen as an unintentional commentary on the pop music industry's tendency to wipe clean any vestige of personal style and replace it with a (theoretically) more marketable image – as happened to Daltrey himself in the early part of his career.

CREDITS

WE ARE GRATEFUL TO THE FOLLOWING, WHO HAVE GIVEN PERMISSION FOR THE USE OF THEIR COPYRIGHT MATERIAL:

A & M RECORDS LTD. p. 20 Shawn Phillips (photo by Sanders Nicholson), p. 74 Shrink (photo by Andra Nelki, Oval), p. 105 Sting (photo by Brian Aris), p. 105 Captain Sensible (photo by Janette Beckman), p. 110 Little Nell (photo by Graham Hughes), p. 124 Joe Jackson's Jumpin' Jive (photo by Anton Corbijn), p. 125 Jools Holland (photo by Jill Furmanovsky), p. 141 'Look Sharp!' (photo by Brian Griffin)
ACE/CHISWICK RECORDS LTD. p. 12 Gorillas, p. 24 Eddie Noack, p. 28 Moods, p. 48 Captain Sensible, p. 52 Dave Vanian, p. 54 Olympics, p. 93 Bal, p. 118 Dynamite Band, p. 121 Ike Turner, p. 137 Jesse Hector
ARISTA p. 18 Showaddywaddy, p. 23 Alannah Currie, p. 32 Showaddywaddy, p. 43 Aretha Franklin, p. 58 April Love, p. 68 Fashion, p. 73 Gary Glitter, p. 80 Jodelles, p. 92 Brian Setzer, p. 99 Three Degrees, p. 110 Dreams, p. 114 Glitter Band, p. 115 Showaddywaddy, p. 117 Barry Manilow, p. 117 Haircut 100, p. 118 Bay City Rollers, p. 124 Patti Smith, p. 132 Monkees
AURA RECORDS LTD. p. 17 Annette Peacock
AVANTGARDE MAGAZINE p. 27 Barbie Wilde
JON BARRACLOUGH p. 96 Johnny Melton of Specimen (clothes © Theresa Coburn 1983)
BEGGARS BANQUET p. 16 Duffo, p. 41 Incantation (photo by Mike Laye), p. 47 The Doll, p. 62 Randy California, p. 87 Gary Numan
TONY BENYON p. 2 cartoon, p. 10 cartoon, p. 51 Elton John ill, p. 144 cartoon
BEVERLEY SISTERS COLLECTION p. 16, p. 54 & p. 117 Beverley Sisters
ADRIAN BOOT p. 23 Bruce Springsteen
TONY BRAINSBY p. 52 Thin Lizzy
BRONZE RECORDS LTD. p. 19 Motorhead, p. 66 Girlschool, p. 69 Kim Goody, p. 112 Motorhead
MIKE BROWNLOW p. 102–3 Shades ill
BUTT RECORDS/GOUGHSOUND LTD. p. 62 Electric Banana
CHARISMA RECORDS p. 60 Malcolm McLaren, p. 75 Peter Gabriel (photo by Armando Gallo), p. 77 Buffalo Gal
CHARLY RECORDS LTD. p. 20 Jock Macdonald (photo by Andrew Large), p. 25 'Elvis, Scotty & Bill', p. 25 Johnny Cash, p. 29 Dave Taylor, p. 82 Gong, p. 93 Dave Taylor, p. 98 Five Keys, p. 124 Manish Boys, p. 137 Little Richard
CHERRY RED RECORDS LTD. p. 22 Marc Bolan
CHRYSALIS RECORDS p. 16 John Keeble, p. 37 Robin Trower, p. 48 Debbie Harry, p. 53 Ian Hunter, p. 62 Debbie Harry, p. 80 Charlie Dore, p. 86 Debbie Harry, p. 98 Chris Cross, p. 109 Neville Staples, p. 122 Debbie Harry, p. 122 Terry Hall, p. 134 Snuky Tate, p. 135 Lynval Golding
DENNIS COCKELL (EXCLUSIVE TATTOOING, LONDON) p. 119 Steve Jones, p. 120 ill.
COMPACT p. 89 Virna Lindt (photo by Sheila Rock), p. 123 Mari Wilson
CREOLE RECORDS LTD. p. 16 Judge Dread
DECCA UK/LONDON RECORDS p. 11 Ann Peebles, p.36 ZZ Top, p. 38 Ebeneezer Obey, p. 44 Chi-lites, p. 48 Max Splodge, p. 50 Roy Orbison, p. 54 Zombies, p. 56 Residents, p. 70 John Mayall, p. 72 Bananarama, p. 73 Ace Cannon, p. 74 Billy Fury, p. 82 Rolling Stones, p. 89 Cruisers, p. 91 Rolling Stones, p. 92 Bobby Rydell, p. 108 Les Rockets, p. 113 Bob Crosby, p. 113 Brian Poole & the Tremeloes, p. 116 Rod Stewart, p. 127 Little Eva, p. 140 Attractions, p. 142 Sylvester
DEMON RECORDS LTD. p. 54 Treniers, p. 116 Escorts, p. 136 Mojos
E. G. p. 131 Bryan Ferry (photo by Eric Boman)

EDSEL/F-BEAT p. 8 Julie London, p. 8 Nick Lowe
EMI RECORDS (UK) p. 17 Mik Sweeney, p. 22 Gina X, p. 48 Marc Bolan, p. 49 Diana Ross, p. 51 Shadows, p. 51 Thomas Dolby, p. 51 John Lennon, p. 52 Gina X, p. 56 Jets, p. 60 John Taylor, p. 60 Sheena Easton, p. 67 Beki Bondage, p. 68 Freddie Mercury, p. 71 David Coverdale, p. 72 Kenny Rogers, p. 76 Fish, p. 84 Plasmatics, p. 88 George Clinton, p. 94 Slim Whitman, p. 96 Wendy O. Williams, p. 98 Steve Van Zandt, p. 104 Sal Solo, p. 108 Klaus Meime, p. 109 Slik, p. 109 Olivia Newton-John, p. 117 Shadows, p. 120 Rolling Stones, p. 122 Limahl, p. 125 Paul McCartney, p. 125 Melba Moore, p. 129 Rolling Stones, p. 131 John King, p. 133 Beatles, p. 134 Duran Duran, p. 135 Cliff Richard, p. 136 Thomas Dolby, p. 137 Kenny Rogers, p. 139 Keith Richard, p. 139 Charlie Watts, p. 139 Cliff Richard, p. 140 Rick Nelson, p. 142 'Sticky Fingers' Front cover Diana Ross.
F-BEAT RECORDS LTD. p. 46 Carlene Carter, p. 51 Elvis Costello, p. 110 Carlene Carter
FLYING FISH RECORDS p. 61 Gove Scrivenor, p. 139 Sam Chatman
CAROLINE GREVILLE-MORRIS p. 96 Adam Ant
ISLAND RECORDS p. 23 Bob Marley, p. 28 Grace Jones, p. 33 Bob Marley, p. 38 Slits, p. 40 Sunny Adé, p. 42 Eno, p. 47 Bryan Ferry, p. 58 Bob Marley, p. 114 Kid Creole, p. 121 B-52's, p. 127 Coconuts, p. 128 Grace Jones
JET RECORDS LTD. p. 110 Girl
JUNGLE RECORDS, LONDON p. 53 Malaria! (photo by Edo)
K-TEL INTERNATIONAL (UK) p. 94 Elvis (ill by Jeff Cummings, album sleeve designed by Acrobat)
LONDON FEATURES INTERNATIONAL p. 66 Marianne Faithfull
MAGNUM FORCE RECORDS Front cover Elvis, p. 52 Gene Vincent, p. 74 Elvis
MCA RECORDS INC. p. 24 Dan Peek, p. 45 Rick Nelson, p. 50 Buddy Holly, p. 53 Waylon Jennings, p. 55 Dream Express, p. 60 Michael Grant, p. 62 Dealer, pp. 65 and 69 Tanya Tucker, p. 71 John Sykes, p. 82 Stargard, p. 97 Jerry Lee Lewis, p. 104 Riff Regan, p. 113 Louis Jordan, p. 124 Joe Ely, p. 126 Gary Moore
MEGATONE RECORDS p. 69 Sarah Dash (photo & make-up by Marc Raboy, clothes by Silicia Farrar, hair by Selita Butler)
MOTOWN RECORDS pp. 11 and 22 Michael Jackson, p. 24 Supremes & Four Tops, p. 30 Temptations, p. 39 Syreeta, p. 43 Supremes, p. 49 Diana Ross, p. 54 Supremes, p. 55 Four Tops, p. 55 Temptations & Supremes, p. 73 Martha & Vandellas, p. 83 Rick James, p. 88 Syreeta, p. 100 Jean Carn, p. 100 Bonnie Pointer, p. 101 Stevie Wonder, p. 101 Tata Vega, p. 121 Mary Wells, p. 131 Four Tops, p. 135 Diana Ross, p. 139 Marvin Gaye
PHONOGRAM p. 11 Rimshots, p. 13 Status Quo, p. 21 Dee. D Jackson, p. 21 Paul Stanley, p. 30 Kevin Rowland, p. 31 Status Quo, p. 33 Marilyn, p. 36 Elton John, p. 49 Stephanie Mills, p. 53 Chuck Berry, p. 55 ABC, p. 56 Ramones, p. 58 Elton John, p. 59 Village People, p. 68 Julian Cope, p. 72 Big Country, p. 73 Martin Fry, p. 77 Kiss, p. 88 Sheila Chandra (photo by Chalkie Davies), p. 91 Fool, p. 97 Donna Summer, p. 100 Esther Phillips, p. 105 Alex Harvey Band, p. 108 Sho-Nuff, p. 109 Junior, p. 110 Ritchie Family, p. 111 Lita Ford, p. 125 Brian Downey, p. 130 New York Dolls, p. 133 Elton John, p. 140 Joneses
PHOTO FEATURES p. 11 Ray Dorset, p. 15 Fee Waybill, p. 20 Scott McKenzie, p. 27 Roy Wood, p. 30 Cher, p. 42 Todd Rundgren, p. 45 Ozzy Osbourne, p. 49 Prince, p. 52 Alvin Stardust, p. 58 Jimi Hendrix, p. 67 Alice Cooper, p. 76 Arthur Brown, p. 79 Adam Ant, p. 81 Cilla Black, p. 85 Peter Quaife, p. 86 Vince Neil, p. 90 Dale Bozzio, p. 93 Billy Fury, p. 95 Liberace, p. 96 Marc Bolan, p. 97 Meatloaf, p. 98 Rod Stewart, p. 99 Tina Turner, p. 106 Lulu, p. 112 Rob Halford, p. 116 Jam, p. 121 Ronettes, p. 126 P. J. Proby, p. 126 Biff, p. 127 Nina Hagen, p. 137 ZZ Top, p. 138 Frank Zappa
PICKWICK RECORDS p. 13 Leo Sayer, p. 22 Donovan, p. 65 Rod Stewart
PLANT LIFE RECORDS LTD. p. 61 Dead Sea Surfers (photo by Buick Photographic)

TED POLHEMUS p. 69 Max, p. 128 Marilyn, p. 130 Ronny, p. 130 Boy George
PRESIDENT RECORDS LTD. LONDON p. 19 Gene Autry, p. 74 Little Richard
PRT RECORDS p. 18 'Do Wop', p. 41 Savanna, p. 57 Kenny Ball, p. 57 George Melly, p. 81 Imagination (courtesy of R & B Records), p. 83 Techno Twins, p. 99 Sequence, p. 113 George Melly, p. 136 Acker Bilk
RADIALCHOICE p. 81 Toni Basil (PR pic for single 'Mickey'), p. 90 Toto Coelo
RAZOR RECORDS LTD. p. 79 Monkey
RCA RECORDS Front cover Bowie, p. 12 Bowie, p. 19 Biff, p. 20 Steve Priest, p. 23 Joboxers, p. 25 Jim Reeves, p. 28 Ann Lennox, p. 28 Crack, p. 30 Peter Kaukonen, p. 33 Eddy Grant, p. 33 Haysi Fantazee, p. 35 Porter Wagoner, p. 35 Hank Snow, p. 35 John Denver, p. 36 Andy Scott, p. 38 Denny Laine, p. 41 Anna, p. 41 Tane Cain, p. 42 Charley Pride, p. 43 Dana Gillespie, p. 45 Bonnie Tyler, p. 45 Grace Slick, p. 45 Dolly Parton, p. 47 Smokey Robinson, p. 47 Annabella Lwin, p. 51 Nana Mouskouri, p. 53 Bix Beiderbecke, p. 57 Slade, p. 57 James Brown, p. 57 Fats Waller, p. 57 Bing Crosby, p. 58 John Denver, p. 58 Willie Nelson, p. 60 Bowie, p. 61 Elvis, p. 62 Celena Duncan, p. 62 Jack Cassady, p. 65 Rick James, p. 65 Bowie, p. 66 Heaven, p. 69 Bliss, p. 70 Sweet, p. 71 Harvey Bainbridge, p. 75 Bowie, p. 75 Annabella Lwin, p. 75 Baccara, p. 76 Bowie, p. 76 Lou Reed, p. 86 Dolly Parton, p. 87 Lou Reed, p. 88 Stevie Wonder, p. 90 Nona Hendryx, p. 94 Porter Wagoner, p. 94 Diana Ross, p. 97 Dottie West, p. 98 War, p. 99 Sylvester, p. 100 Sylvie Vartan, p. 101 Graham Parker, p. 104 Isaac Hayes, p. 105 Diana Ross, p. 106 Claudia Barry, p. 107 Bowie, p. 107 Bow Wow Wow, p. 107 Kate Garner, p. 108 Landscape, p. 109 Beggar & Co., p. 112 Lou Reed, p. 114 Bowie, p. 117 Commodores, p. 119 Rose Tattoo, p. 121 Velvelettes, p. 125 Klaus Nomi, p. 127 Kate Robbins, p. 127 Bonnie Tyler, p. 128 Bowie, p. 130 Anne Lennox, p. 131 Motams, p. 132 Elvis, p. 136 One The Juggler, p. 137 Thelonious Monk, p. 138 Martin Griffin, p. 140 Four Tops
RICHARD ROBSON ASSOCIATES, p. 16 Chas & Dave, p. 19 Grandmaster Flash, p. 56 Darts, p. 104 Buster Bloodvessel, p. 125 Stargazers
RIVA RECORDS LTD. p. 30 John Cougar Mellencamp
RONCO (TELEPRODUCTS) LTD. p. 48 Frankie Laine
ANDY ROSEN Front cover John Lydon, p. 118 John Lydon
SAFARI RECORDS pp. 26 and 78 Toyah, p. 128 Jayne County
SCHMALTZ p. 68 Steve Strange (photo by Eugene Adebari), p. 79 Steve Strange (photo by Robyne Beeche), p. 134 Steve Strange (photo by Helmut Newton)
SECRET RECORDS/PANACHE MUSIC p. 27 Exploited, p. 46 Dee Snider, p. 66 Infa Riot, p. 67 'Secret Life of Punks', p. 76 Dee Snider, p. 104 Wattie, p. 111 'Britannia Waives The Rules', p. 122 Gonads, p. 135 Glynn Barber
SOZYAMUDA RECORDS p. 84 Sic F*cks
RAY STEVENSON p. 89 Siouxsie
STIFF RECORDS p. 12 Madness, p. 17 Ian Dury, p. 23 Madness, p. 37 Brigit Novik, p. 41 Jane Aire, p. 58 Madness, p. 81 Jennie McKeown, p. 88 Lene Lovich, p. 91 Rumour, p. 106 Tracey Ullman, p. 107 Wendy O. Williams & Lemmy, p. 116 Madness Logo, p. 124 Judy of Bellestars, p. 134 Eddie Tudorpole
SUFFER FOR THEIR ART RECORDS p. 38 Access
SURVIVAL RECORDS p. 82 Tik & Tok pic disc (photo by Alastair Hughes, hair by Sanrizz)
TRINIFOLD LTD. p. 46 Roger Daltrey, p. 48 Keith Moon, p. 85 'Quadrophenia', p. 130 Eric Clapton & Keith Moon, p. 142 Roger Daltrey
TROJAN RECORDINGS LTD. p. 34 Big Youth
VIRGIN RECORDS LTD. Front cover Boy George, p. 56 Devo, p. 58 Devo, p. 78 David Sylvian, p. 78 Boy George
VISTA SOUNDS (The specialists in reggae, soul & disco music) p. 114 'Soul-Ska!'
WEA RECORDS LTD. p. 87 Bette Bright, p. 104 Psychic TV
WHALEY-MALIN PRODUCTIONS LTD. p. 84 Jordan

143

ACKNOWLEDGEMENTS

SPECIAL THANKS TO:
The *New Musical Express* advertising dept, Leslie Gardner, Transformer, Virgin Megastore, 'Luigi & The Boys' record shop, Dennis Cockell, Mike Brownlow, Andy Warren, Jade Starr, Lisa Cooper, Kwik Copy/Pip NW6, Jean-Mathis Fritsch, Angela Coles, Josie & Rick Britt, Tony Riley, Roxy Meade, Michael Rubinstein, Andre Csillag, David Wainwright, Chalkie Davies, Gill Smith, Theresa Coburn, Carol Fawcett, Hugh Birley, Gem Howard, Jamie Spencer, Sue Skeats, Richard Routledge, David Short, Dave Archer, Jock Macdonald, Brian Southall, Oliver Drake, Sue Humphris, Magenta de Vine, everyone at Trinifold, Roger Daltrey, Sue Johns, Julia Marcus, Paul Kinder, Andrew Lauder, Jean Luc Young, Joop Visser, Fiona Grimshaw, The Beverley Sisters, Ceri Nicholas, Lee Ellen Nauman, Tony Benyon, Petra Elkan, Simon Porter, Shelagh Macleod, Nicholas Clark, Ray Stevenson, Eric Jackson (IPC), Adrian Boot, Andy Rosen, Boy George, Marilyn, Charlie Gillett, Flicknife, Rialto, 4AD, Everest, Relic, On-U, DJM, Magnet, Land of Giants, Satril, Julian Henry, Albion, Liz Cruickshanks, Gerry Denn, Robin Parry, Nick Tracken, our families, Cori & Nicky, Cherry Red and all the music paper advertisers, their writers and artists

REFERENCE BOOKS:
The Illustrated Rock Handbook (Salamander Books), *The Sound Of The City* by Charlie Gillett (Souvenir Press), *The Guinness Book Of Hit Singles, The Rock Yearbook* (Virgin Books), *Cool Cats* by Tony Stewart (Eel Pie), *The Rolling Stone Record Guide* (Virgin Books), *The Rock Star Tattoo Encyclopedia* by Patricia Steur (Plastic), *Music and Video Week Directory* (Music Week Ltd.), *Shout! The True Story of The Beatles*, by Philip Norman (Corgi).

The authors have made every effort to obtain clearance for the use of photographs, record sleeves and advertisements. In a very few instances where these attempts were fruitless, the authors will be pleased to hear from those concerned.

Front cover
Clockwise from top right:
David Bowie as 'Aladin Sane'
John Lydon of Public Image Ltd. (ex-Johnny Rotten of The Sex Pistols)
Boy George of Culture Club on 'Karma Chameleon'
Elvis Presley in classic 1950s pose on 'The King Is Dead'
Diana Ross on 'Why Do Fools Fall in Love?'

Back cover
Clockwise from top right:
Detail of Kahn & Bell ad from SOUNDS, 1980
Junex ruffled shirt ad from NME, 1965
Detail of Husklynn Ltd. drainpipe jeans ad in SOUNDS, 1980
Detail of Gerald Manleigh of Oxford St. Western shirt ad in NME, 1952
'Star Album' jewellery detail from Prelude Jewellery Ltd. ad in NME, 1963
Detail of Denson winklepickers ad from NME, 1964

'Trendy' leather waistcoat detail from Branded Discounts Ltd. ad in NME, 1970
Detail of Carnaby Cavern ad from NME, 1969
Centre: Detail of studded wristband from Printout Promotions ad in SOUNDS, 1982

Page 1
Detail of collarless 'Beatle Jacket' ad from Aburtrim Ltd. DISC, 1964

Page 2
Tony Benyon cartoon from NME, 1973

Page 3
Left: Detail of Chandleys ad from NME, 1964
Top right: Detail from M. & B. Supplies ad in NME, 1965
Bottom right: Detail from Granny's Emporium ad in NME, 1967

Tony Benyon cartoon from NME, 1974